Adirondack L

The Illustrated Life of Richard ~~~ ᴜᴜᴜ
1895-1977

By Scot H. Dahms

Author of
E.J. Dailey: The Last Adirondack Trapper, 1889-1973
Walter A. Gibbs: Ohio Trains, Triumph Traps & Maryland Muskrats, 1869-1941

Adirondack Dick Enterprises:

Trapping Antiques, Vintage Photography, Editing, Publishing
2270 W Willow Lane, Peru, Indiana 46970
ranger1971@comcast.net

For Sarah

Thanks go to Rich Braun, Jeff Bowman, Brad Cords and Gary Riemenschneider for photographs and/or information. Special thanks to Tom Parr for supporting my research in the Trap Museum. Thanks also go to Boyd and Susan Dahms for assisting with editing and research.

Contents

Foreword

A brief overview of Dick's life was previously included in the Trap Collector's Guide, Second Edition, published in early 2016. Because of deadlines and space restrictions, the article was more of an overview of his life. I wanted to create a more thorough history of this man highlighting the many positive impacts he had on the world. This book is my contribution to his legacy.

Best known in the trap collecting community for his work with the Triumph Trap Company and his escapades with Elric J. "E.J." Dailey in the Adirondacks, Richard K. "Dick" Wood greatly influenced the outdoor writing and photography community as well. Early in his career, his articles mainly graced the copies of the Triumph Trap Company literature and the magazine called Fur News, which was later called Fur News and Outdoor World.

Dick's articles told stories of his country wide trapping adventures or specifics on catching all types of furbearer species. Many of his articles included references to Daniel Boone, sourdough trappers or the finding of some kind of mecca.

Research for this book led me to read many of Dick's articles – over 300 in total. Although I may not have used information from all of them in this book, I have listed them at the end in chronological order for those interested in mapping his progression as a writer. I know that I do not have all of them. If you happen to find one that I do not have, I would appreciate it if you would send me a copy.

Articles from other sources are provided in chronological order as well. I referenced many E.J. Dailey articles as Dick and E.J. shared many experiences on the trap line. I used a very basic system for documenting references: article name, department (if needed), name of publication, name of author and date.

This book is a compilation of Dick's stories and escapades written in his words as much as possible. I compressed his stories to maximize space but also tried to use the same terminology as he did. I tried to put his articles together in a cohesive format which I hope you enjoy. At times, Dick would combine fiction and nonfiction. I tried to include only nonfiction.

If I could put Dick at a specific location on a specific day, I included the date as Dick included dates on some of his articles. In a few instances, Dick published the same general story with different details in different magazines years apart. My impression was that the article published earlier was more factual as sometimes impressive details were added to the second publishing of the story. This made me question why that information was not included the first time the story was published.

Later in life, he focused more on his first love of photography and wrote articles focusing on that. His photographs are published in many books, magazines and brochures dating from 1915 to today.

All photographs in this book were taken by Dick unless otherwise noted. Most included are high resolution scans of original photographs. In a very few cases, high resolution scans from newspapers and magazines were utilized. Photographs were not touched up in any way, so the reader will see less than perfect images in some instances.

Dick made a couple of interesting comments about the collection of antiques. In 1924, Dick thought that those who had a collection of antique books on Western Americana, not only had an interesting library, but also had a profitable investment. Dick believed that books about Western Americana were becoming scarcer and more valuable each year. I bet most collectors have heard a similar comment about antiques.

Another comment of particular interest to antique trap collectors was from a 1971 letter. In this letter, Dick responds to an inquiry about him writing a book on the history of the steel trap. Dick asked the question, "Would there be enough interest, or market, for such a work?"

As you read through this book, you will find comments made by Dick long ago which came true. Dick was a forward thinker always busy with improving himself.

Dick in his house at Red Bank, Tennessee.

Chapter 1. The Early Years

Dick's father, George Spurgeon Wood

Dick was born on June 15, 1895 in Scott County, Virginia. He was the oldest son to George Spurgeon Wood, a Methodist "circuit-rider" preacher, and Isabelle (Belle) Hart Wood. George and Belle were married on August 3, 1893. They belonged to the Methodists of the Holston Conference.

The Sketches of Holston Preachers document provided the following description of George. "He was one of those patient, faithful itinerants, who served hard charges without complaint, lived frugally, worked loyally, kept out of debt, loved his work, honored his church, and in every field where he labored, held the confidence of his own people and the esteem of others."

Dick's grandfather, Henry L. Wood, was a minister in the Methodist Episcopal Church, South. Although his grandfather died before his birth, both his father and grandfather being ministers had an impact on where Dick later chose to attend school.

Prior to the fall of 1909, the family relocated to Pond Creek in east central Tennessee where Dick saw his first automobile. It was a Maxwell with a flat top trunk behind the front seat. The car arrived during church services on a Sunday and the entire congregation turned out to see it.

Dick's interest in trapping and the outdoors was fueled by reading several trapping books at a young age including Hill's "Life of Daniel Boone" and Abbott's "Kit Carson". At the age of fourteen, Dick was attracted to trapping due to the high prices paid at the time. Muskrats were bringing $0.50, opossum $1, skunk $5 and mink $6. His first trap line was along Pond Creek. Dick had problems catching his first animal but finally caught a muskrat. He purchased a pair of hip waders, increased the number of traps he had, and increased his line to ten miles of creek bank with several loops through the bluffs for skunk and possum. Each morning he usually caught a few muskrats and an occasional possum or skunk.

Another trapper named Eli Fox moved into the neighborhood and set out an extended line along both sides of Pond Creek. The trapping area was Eli's by right of first claim, but Eli never bothered Dick's traps. Eli was very kind and showed Dick how to make sets. Eli spent all his time along the creek. His specialty was mink trapping.

Eli boarded near Dick's home, so Dick routinely went to see him after supper. Eli shared his experiences about trapping and hunting, including adventures in the Smoky Mountains. With the rising price of mink, Dick's interest in catching this animal increased. Eli shared that he used mostly blind sets for mink.

With the new knowledge, Dick was sure he would catch a bunch of mink. Unfortunately, he did not catch one until December. He caught it in a spring water set. This catch provided a kick start to his waning enthusiasm. Instead of going just a quarter or a half a day, Dick planned to set out enough traps to occupy all his time from morning to night.

Eli decided to vacate the territory. Eli willingly showed Dick all his paying sets over a few mornings. Dick gleaned as much information as he could from Eli's fifty years of experience. Eli showed him paths under bridges and over bluffs along with cut across points of land that were regularly travelled by mink. There were a few sets which were sure to catch a mink every few days. Dick found tributaries he did not know existed. Eli shared that these tributaries were ideal places to catch mink and raccoon. Eli also shared muskrat feeding places, ponds and sloughs.

To top it off, Eli offered to share his special scent base, fish oil, and lent Dick as many of his traps as he could use. Eli liked under spring traps because of their compactness and light weight. He used them exclusively. Dick selected twenty-five of Eli's best traps to use.

Later in life, Dick said his favorite furbearer to trap was the mink. I believe this was fostered by Eli's instruction. Dick also said that the mink in the Holston River area were the slyest and most difficult to catch.

This photograph of Dick was used in the article titled "Trapping for Muskrats – and Getting Them" in the September 1917 issue of Fur News.

Dick used Eli's best sets on both sides of the creek. The additional territory extended the line by three miles on each end of the original ten miles. Dick checked some traps every other day. He checked the traps next to the settled areas daily to reduce issues with dogs, cows and farm help. With the additional territory, Dick walked twelve to fifteen miles a day.

The number of animals that Dick caught each day increased substantially. He skinned them as he checked his line. He was now catching at least a mink a day with more skunks and raccoon. He stretched all the animals on boards he personally whittled.

By the middle of December, Dick had caught two hundred muskrats. He took all his traps and now focused on land animals including skunk, raccoon and opossum. In the area he trapped, there were several trees that had been blown over by storms. Usually, the exposed root balls held a family of skunks. He was lucky as every skunk was a star black which were the ones most coveted.

Dick sold his furs before Christmas and placed $100 of the proceeds in a local bank. He then took a few days off to hunt ducks and rabbits. After the holidays, Dick moved to Sweetwater Creek to locate new trapping ground. He found numerous muskrats and mink not previously disturbed by other trappers. Dick planned to move into a shack and had his equipment moved there. The number of furbearers caught daily on the Pond Creek trap line decreased and there was starting to be some theft of traps and animals, so the change in location was welcomed.

Starting in January of 1910, Dick lived in the shack alone for three months. He slept on a cot and made his own meals. The windows were broken, so he was practically sleeping in the open air. Dick learned that exercise, wholesome food and fresh air are the secrets of good health as he never was sick. This experience would serve him well when he trapped in the Adirondacks.

Dick was checking a hundred traps a day and was up at first light everyday. He quit trapping land animals the first of February. He then trapped muskrats for two months and caught his first otter at a nearby pond. It brought $12. Dick started pulling his traps on the first of April. His largest catch of the season was made on the day he was leaving. He resolved to return to the Sweetwater and Pond Creek areas the next year, but he never trapped them again.

Dick's parents greeted him as though he had been gone for years. The local trappers were impressed with his large catch and asked what type of lure he was using. When Dick told them he used blind sets, the other trappers thought he was trying to hide what lure he was using.

Dick sold his furs and received over $200. The question was what would be purchased with it. He wanted a motorcycle but knew there would not be enough left after he bought his summer fishing supplies and traps for next season.

Dick's parents saw his trapping ability but could not see spending so much money on "foolishness". They discouraged trapping and, believed if he went down that road, he would "grow up in ignorance". His father had offered to pay for Dick to go to advanced schooling. Dick had no interest in a scholastic career and told his former school mates in the "free school" goodbye. His old-school mates would give him a pitying smile and wondered if Dick was "off" in the head.

Robert Guy Barnes, Dick's first best friend from the "free school", had continued to the ninth grade and, while beginning the school year in September of 1909, inquired about what school Dick was going to attend. At that time, he had already decided to trap for that season and not go to school. Dick noted that this friend died before 1920 from a flu epidemic

Dick's parents were unrelenting in their wish that he continue school beyond the eighth grade. He finally changed his mind and used the money from trapping for school. Dick did not want his parents making sacrifices on his account.

Although Dick said he did not get a motorcycle with his trapping money, he did get one at some point.

Dick sitting at his father's desk.

In 1910, Dick went to Madisonville, Tennessee to take high school level classes on the campus of Hiwassee College. At that time, Hiwassee College was jointly operated by the trustees of the college and the Holston Conference of the Methodist Episcopal Church – South. There was a building on the campus for non-college students. After completing the four-year curriculum, he received a Bachelor in Science High School Degree. Back then, educational program terminology was not standardized and this program should not be confused with a modern Bachelor of Science from a university. This program was not equivalent to a high school diploma so he had to attend an established high school to get a high school diploma. Taking this program resulted in Dick graduating from high school just one month short of his 21st birthday.

While attending the school on Hiawassee College's campus, Dick's instructors would preach specialization in any field a student chose to enter. The story often told to reinforce this was about the town-hall clock repairman getting fifty-five dollars for his work. Five was for doing the work and fifty was for knowing how. In 1934, Dick commented that the jack-of-all-trades did better during the Great Depression.

Dick with Herbert Webster at Umbrella Rock on Lookout Mountain, Chattanooga, Tennessee, 1915. Herbert was from New Hope in the Pond Creek Valley of Tennessee.

In 1913, Dick's family relocated to Hixson, Tennessee just north of Chattanooga. Dick wrote an article about two friends and him exploring the Chickamauga Creek area while living at Hixson. He published two articles about this adventure. One was titled "Trout, Wildcats and Rattlesnakes" published in two parts in the July and September 1918 issues of Fur News. The other article was titled "Back of Horseshoe Bend" in Sportsman's Digest in 1929.

Both articles basically had the same course of events with some details from the 1918 article left out and some new details added in the 1929 article. One noted difference between the two was they carried different firearms on the trip. I included the firearms from the first article because I think the firearms from the second article were changed to add extra interest. One notable change in the guns was the inclusion of a 10-gauge shotgun. Another notable difference in the

12

second article was a photograph of southwest Virginia in a story about southern Tennessee.

One November while living at Hixson, Dick along with "Dilsie" and the "Kid" headed for the Barker Camp located near the mouth of Chickamauga Gulch. They each rode a horse and had two more to carry duffle plus grub. They would leave their horses there and walk to the head of Chickamauga Creek. Dilsie had herded cattle on the free range for years and knew the country well. Dick and the Kid were making their first trip into the area. Dick wanted to verify the tales of "trout galore" and bear sign.

The three were highly concerned about rattlesnakes so they came prepared. Dilsie and the Kid had three quarts of liquor with them in case of snake bites. Dick only had a small flask full. Rattlesnakes were the only drawback to mountain life. It necessitated the wearing of stiff, uncomfortable leggings and carrying of many quarts of snake medicine.

Dick described Dilsie as a typical Southern mountaineer who had experience in every sort of outdoor work there was including logging, coal mining, moon shining and even night riding for excitement. Dilsie was content to remain as long as the coffee and snake remedy lasted. If either became exhausted, Dilsie would leave. Dilsie never had a pressing duty when a trip into the mountains was proposed.

Clarence Skelton – the Kid. This picture was used in the article titled "Lake Fishing" in the September 1918 issue of Fur News.

The Kid was younger and given to devilish pranks being a bold and free East Tennessean. He managed a well-regulated farm and by choice helped Dilsie herd cattle on the mountain. The Kid was a favorite of the local mountain men. He had aristocratic parentage and was blessed with the luxuries of life. The Kid's greatest pleasure was being out with the rough, carefree people that managed to make a scant living in the mountains by herding cattle and sheep. He herded during the summer, picked huckleberries in the fall and trapped in the winter. The Kid usually accompanied Dick on hunting trips.

Dick utilized the caption "You have to lie on your back to see the noon day sun" to describe this photo which was in the article titled "Back of Horseshoe Bend" in the Sportsman's Digest magazine. This photo was taken in southwest Virginia but the article was about an area by Hixson, Tennessee.

Dick looking off the top of Walden's Ridge. Note the leggings worn for protection against snakes. Dick commented that they were stiff and uncomfortable.

Dick looking off Walden's Ridge several years later.

Dick suggested to the Kid that they take a week off and just ramble along, taking it easy with the goal of reaching the head of Chickamauga Gulch. Dilsie readily agreed to come along for food and a dollar a day. That was a good wage in that locality.

They reached the foot of Walden's Ridge and stopped to fill their canteens. They also tightened the saddle girths for the mile climb and followed the narrow foot trail leading toward Barker Camp.

Dick with "Prince", the family horse.

Upon arrival, they put the horses in the enclosed lot to graze. The camp had an old, dilapidated building occasionally used by cattlemen. They found the building occupied by some semi-wild goats that did not want to leave. Dick and the Kid each grabbed a horn and drug the Billy goat out and the rest followed.

Dilsie gathered a supply of wood while Dick and the Kid cleaned the camp. The Kid took ahold of the corner of bedding in a bunk and heard the warning of a rattler's buzzing tail. The snake flopped on the floor. Dilsie came in and killed the snake with a short pole. As the Kid pulled the bedding off the bunk, two more rattlers hit the ground and were promptly shot.

At an hour before sundown, they shouldered their firearms to shoot some squirrels to eat. Dick carried a .22 rifle, Dilsie a .32-20 Smith & Wesson revolver and the Kid had a .44 Colt.

The three left early the next morning. By 11:00 am the next day, they had gone five miles. They saw some roosting turkeys, but the turkeys flew away far before the three could get a shot.

At 3:00 pm, the three heard a creaking and groaning from above. They looked up to see a tree fall from a cliff right above them. They dashed under a rock overhang and watched the tree hit right where they had been standing. The tree was partially rotted and exploded into several pieces upon impact. Even rotted, it could have hurt them very badly and they were a good distance from any type of help.

They built a shelter and sleeping bunk before dark. The bunk was above the ground and had room for all three. Dick commented that no one sleeps on the ground in snake country.

Dick awoke with a startled feeling that something was wrong. Rain was pouring down in torrents, and it was lightening and thundering terrifically. All around, Dick heard the roaring of water. He placed his feet over the edge of the bunk and down into a foot of water. Dick moved his feet toward the head of the bunk where it was higher and placed them down right on a rattle snake. He let out a yell and rammed his head against the low roof of the shelter.

Dick ramming his head dumped water down onto Dilsie and the Kid. They both wondered what was going on. Dick informed them that they were surrounded by water and were sharing the shelter with at least one rattlesnake.

This bit of information sparked life into both Dilsie and the Kid. Dilsie began groping around in the dark for either the flashlight or the medicine bottle. The Kid took off, leaving a hole in the shelter wall where he went through. Dick and Dilsie followed through the same hole. The three got together on high ground to discuss their predicament.

The rainstorm came up suddenly and dumped on the headwaters of the waterway which had been a small stream when they went to sleep. The almost dry stream was now a raging torrent. Dilsie took the flashlight and rescued the blankets and whatever else he could from the shelter. They took shelter under a rock ledge for the rest of the night.

The next morning, the stream had subsided to about its normal capacity. All that remained of the shelter was the up-rights and ridgepole. Upon resuming their trip, they found numerous rattlesnakes which had been killed by the high water.

At 11:00, they stopped at a deep pool to fish for trout. Unfortunately, they found that the hooks had been lost in the flood. The Kid suggested shooting at the visible fish in the pool. The shots resulted in no hits. They realized they had to aim about 8 inches low to hit the fish. The three wasted a bunch of lead by trial and error before hitting them. They finally learned to climb out on limbs overhanging the pool and shoot straight down to increase their accuracy.

In the middle of the afternoon, they figured they were eighteen miles from the mouth of the Gulch. That was six miles further than they had ever gone. Dilsie knew of a small log cabin at the head of Hixson Creek that had been built by some hunters. However, there was no trail to follow so the remaining trip was extremely difficult.

Dick, Dilsie and the Kid arrived at Hixson Creek below the cabin. As they came around the bend of the creek, they saw a wild hog. Dilsie and the Kid got into shooting positions as they had the larger guns. Dick, with the smaller gun, drove the hogs to the others.

Dilsie saw twelve hogs running at him and opened up at thirty feet with his .32-20 Smith & Wesson. His shots routed another bunch of wild hogs which ran right toward the Kid. The Kid was surprised by the hogs and, instead of shooting, climbed a cliff at record breaking speed. Dilsie and Dick both shot a hog.

Dilsie and the Kid took turns carrying one hog. As they rounded a corner, Dilsie put his foot down within six inches of a rattlesnake. The snake struck at Dilsie, but it glanced off his legging. Both Dilsie and the Kid shot it. The snake had nineteen rattles. The snake contaminated one hog so they were not able to dress it. The other hog was dressed immediately and hung on the ridge pole on the end of the cabin.

While straightening up a bunk, Dick found a rattlesnake. It was quickly dispatched and the entire cabin was searched for others. After giving it the twice over, they deemed it safe for one night. Unfortunately, they would have another issue to deal with this night.

About 2:00 am, they were awakened by growls and snarls right over their heads. Two wildcats were fighting over the pork in the cabin rafters. During the fight, the cats were on the ends of some boards and all tumbled down into the cabin – boards, cats and all. Dick, Dilsie and the Kid climbed on top of a rafter. Dilsie had grabbed his gun before heading into the rafters and fired on the cats.

One of the cats was killed and the other secured refuge where it could not be found. Dick, Dilsie and the Kid decided it was better to stay in the rafters for the night. In the morning, they found the other cat had left.

Dick crosses Chickamauga Creek on a tree. The photo was used in the article titled "Back of Horseshoe Bend" in Sportsman's Digest magazine.

The next day they hunted in the flat area covered by white oaks on the other side of Chickamauga Creek. To improvise a bridge across the creek, they cut a tree to span the stream. The three crawled across the tree to decrease the chances of taking a dunking. Dick went first and as he reached the other side, a rooster pheasant jumped up on a log to survey the intruding party. Dick shot it and was the first to bag game that day. By the time they had walked through the stand of oaks, they had harvested fourteen fox squirrels.

The liquor went fast and they were losing interest in staying in the reptile and varmint infested country. They reached the Barker Camp that afternoon. During the rest of the week, Dilsie worked hard to bag a Tom turkey, but did not have any luck. He arrived at camp one evening and conveyed that he had finally found the tree where the turkey was roosting. After dark, the three left camp with the intention of shooting the turkey from its roost.

As they neared the tree, the Kid's loudness became a factor. Dilsie told him to stay in place. Dick and Dilsie continued until they were below the tree looking for the turkey. They saw it in the top of the tree. Dilsie shot, but it did not fall. The Kid could be heard laughing where he was instructed to stay. Upon closer inspection, they found it was a squirrel's nest. When the gun fired, they heard something fly from another tree close in the area. After this setback, they loafed the week away.

Dick with his first cousins, Herbert Hart and Hattie Kate Hart along with Ruby Wood, his sister, after his father died.

George, Dick's father, died on April 24, 1915, while Dick was attending Hixson High School. After his death, Belle, his mother, moved to southwest Virginia with Dick's siblings – Stewart, Ruby and Nell. Belle's family owned property in that area and she was given 10 acres on which to build a house. The property was a mile outside of Hiltons on the Holston River.

Dick with his Hixson High School classmates.

Dick boarded with a family and stayed in the Chattanooga area until he graduated on May 10th, 1916 from Hixson High School. After graduation, Dick tried to adjust to jobs in a nearby city but found the outdoor urge too strong. He returned, via train, to the family farm on the north fork of the Holston River by Hiltons, Virginia.

Dick's mother's farm at Hiltons, Virginia.

Chapter 2. Triumph Trap Company

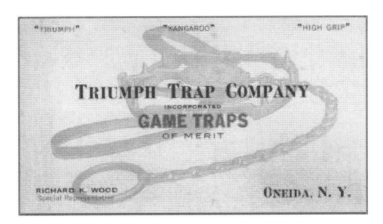

In November of 1916, Dick trapped muskrats on the Holston River. He set six, #1 sized traps. The next day, he had three muskrats and three muskrat feet from escapees. Dick figured either he needed to get some #1 ½ size traps or work on a losing basis.

Dick with a morning's catch of muskrats from the Holston River. This photograph was used on the cover of the September 1917 issue of Fur News.

Dick happened to be looking through the Fur News that evening and saw an advertisement for the Triumph Trap Company. He ordered six traps in various sizes including three High Grip traps. He set them the day after their arrival and ended up having better luck. Dick wrote the article with the above information after he had been hired by the Triumph Trap Company. It was the first article where he included Triumph traps in the message. It would not be the last.

Dick before leaving Hiltons, Virginia for Oneida, New York.

In April of 1917, Dick won a photo contest promoted by the Triumph Trap Company. He did not know he won until he received the $50 check in the mail. The contest was advertised in outdoor magazines including Fur News and Hunter Trader Trapper, but the results were only reported in Hunter Trader Trapper. All photographs were submitted to the managing editor of Hunter Trader Trapper who impartially judged each entry on its merits based on how well it conformed to the contest conditions and showed the appearance of a natural catch.

The winning photograph.

Triumph extended an invitation for Dick to visit them in Oneida. The company provided a $50 expense check. He traveled by train to the interview. When he left New York Central Station, Dick paid the extra fare for a parlor coach with a bar. He took along a steamer trunk packed with all his belongings. It made an impression and he was hired.

The visit resulted in him joining the company's advertising department as a copy writer, photographer and field specialist. This provided him an opportunity to travel throughout the United States including the Maryland marshlands, the Adirondacks, and the Upper Peninsula of Michigan. His duties were to test new traps, report on their efficiency, photograph trappers and fur catches, and furnish any material suitable for publicity and catalog use.

From left to right are Frances E. "Frank" Adams, Dick, Albert E. "Bob" Kinsley and Harry attending a meeting in the Triumph Trap Factory.

Winning this contest was the biggest event in his young career and provided a launching point into the outdoor writing and photography field. He wrote numerous articles and brochures for Triumph including Trapping Tricks, Gripping the Dollars and Modern Trapping Methods.

During his time with Triumph, Dick met Raymond Smiley Spears. This meeting was the beginning of a mentoring relationship between Raymond and Dick. Although Raymond was the mentor, he still learned from Dick. For instance, Raymond said he learned to remove human odor from traps utilizing a method he learned from Dick. Dick buried traps in black muck of a marsh or spring for several weeks prior to trapping season. The traps came out of the muck coated with a dark color. The only smell left on the traps was a mucky smell that did not frighten animals.

In October of 1917, Dick sent Raymond a complete set of Triumph traps. Raymond chose to set the 415 and 415X for bear. A couple of weeks later he caught two bears. Raymond took the bears with the traps still on their paws to the Triumph Trap Factory in Oneida so the makers could look at their traps after the catch. Holdridge Greene, Frances E. Adams and Albert E. "Bob" Kinsley came

26

This photograph was used on the cover of the Triumph Gripping the Dollars booklet. The older gentleman is Mr. Hommel from the Hiltons, Virginia area. The boy is William Homer Hart who is one of Dick's cousins.

Although very similar to the photograph used on the cover of the Gripping the Dollars booklet, this photograph has some small differences.

This Photo was used in the 1918 and 1919 Trapping Tricks.

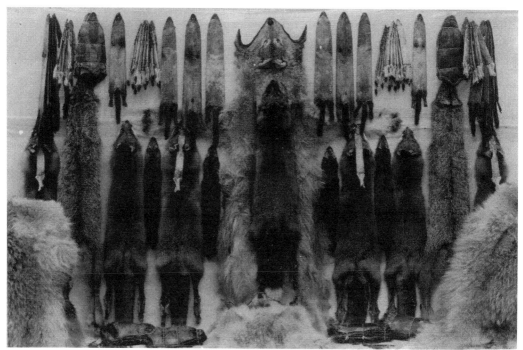

This photograph was used in the Modern Trapping Methods booklet.

Based on the photograph above, a person would have thought it was taken indoors. The trapper was from British Columbia.

out to look at the traps and bears. The traps showed no ill effects from holding the bears. Raymond wrote a story about this in the December 1917 issue of Fur News.

In the winter of 1917, Dick visited Raymond at his camp in the Adirondacks north of the East Branch of West Canada Creek. Dick gave him two little Kangaroo traps. Shortly after this, an express package arrived at Raymond's office. Dick sent him a box of early samples of the smallest Triple Clutch traps. Raymond would later use them for martin.

Barrel of longsprings not complete traps, held in the set position.

Raymond visited the Triumph Trap Factory again in November of 1918. He commented that they had a big factory, an army of experts, a cluster of pretty girls, machines, stamps, barrels of stock, tubs, and chemical treatments. Raymond saw the entire operation from furnace to finished product. He held a Triple Clutch Patent Kangaroo in his hand and was impressed with everything used to make that one trap.

These photographs were taken at John Spears' house at Little Falls, New York in 1923. John was Raymond Spears' father and had a chicken farm on Fairfield Road north of town. The photo on the left was taken by Raymond while the one on the right was taken by Dick.

One of Dick's closest friends while working at the Triumph Trap Factory was Albert E. "Bob" Kinsley. Dick described him as rotund and jolly. He also described him as a rebel from the Oneida Community.

Dick called this photograph "The Veteran Trapper". It was used on the cover of the December 8, 1923 issue of the American Agriculturist. The trapper was Mr. Green from Madison County, New York.

In the summer of 1917, the Triumph Trap Company sent E.J. Dailey complimentary High Grip traps which he used that fall. In January of 1918, E.J. received some Triple Clutch traps and used them that spring. E.J. was very impressed with their effectiveness in catching muskrats. Dick would come to know E.J. very well from their time together in the Adirondacks.

This photograph of Mr. Green was used on the back of the Gripping the Dollars booklet.

In the fall of 1917, Dick trapped with Bill Randall in the Boreas River area of the Adirondack Mountains. Bill made his living trapping, fur buying and commercial fishing through the ice of Lake Champlain. He bought fish from others, combined them with his catch and shipped them to Boston or New York. In the spring, Bill, with hired assistants, caught several hundred muskrats from the marshes around Lake Champlain.

Bill caught fifty to sixty fox the first two months of every season. He used an automobile to trap along roads early in the season. By the middle of November, an attic room in his house was filled with fine fox skins. Later in the season, he would move back into the mountains and trap from a cabin.

This photograph of Bill Randall was used in the article titled "With Randall on the Boreas, Part I" in the February 1918 issue of Fur News.

Bill had a hundred or more double spring fox traps of the jump pattern with medium sized pans. Each had six foot lengths of chain attached to a three-prong grapple. Each trap pan was adjusted to spring hard. Bill used mainly three sets for fox: the spring hole set, the dryland bait set and the blind trail set.

Dick met Bill Randall in the spring of 1917 while on business in Crown Point, New York. Bill invited Dick to trap with him during the 1917 season. This was Dick's first exposure to trapping in the Adirondacks.

Bill had trapped in that foothills area most of his sixty-five years of life. For a certain part of every season, he drove forty miles back into the mountains of the Boreas River area. Bill checked traps along this forty mile trail as he would go back and forth between the camp and getting supplies in town. Although they could use a Ford car to get back to the camp, the traps had to be run by foot or boat from the camp.

The beginning of October, Dick arrived at the train station. Bill met him there and introduced himself. Dick was impressed with Bill's over six foot weather beaten frame and smiling face but thought he was gruff.

The camp was very crude with bunks filled with balsam boughs. During the first night, Dick felt like he was sleeping across railroad ties. Inside of a week, he was hitting the bunk and sleeping with no problems.

On the first night there, a rain storm caused problems with the stove pipe, and it became disconnected. They tried to fix the pipe several times but it usually resulted in a smoke filled cabin. Finally the storm abated, Dick and Bill fixed the stove pipe and got some rest.

The issue with the pipe reminded Dick that the first night in every new camp was memorable. Once while camping in an abandoned cattle camp in the Sand Mountains, he was kept up all night by semi-wild hogs sharpening their tusks on the cabin supports under the floor. Dick commented that night was a miserable one filled with grunts and groans

Dick was not very impressed with Bill's food selection of mainly potatoes, beans and corn bread. The two vegetables were usually hashed brown together in a skillet and dished out. They ate cold lunches and occasionally some bacon with cold pancakes. Dick said that if a waiter had given him that grub at a restaurant, he would have knifed him.

For the first two weeks, Dick and Bill did preseason work including building set locations, scouting for sign and getting traps in order. During the middle of the month, they spent a few days hunting to provide themselves food and bait for cubby pen sets. They each shot a deer. On October 20, it snowed and Bill said it was time to start trapping fox.

Once it got colder, they moved back to the cabin and ran three separate trap lines. The cabin was located at the mouth of Trout Brook on the Boreas River. The first line ran up Trout Brook to the mouth of Durgin Brook. Then it followed Durgin Brook to Sand Pond Mountain, went across to Wolf Pond, then to the Boreas River at the dam and back down to camp.

Beaver hut on Wolf Pond near the Boreas River. Dick did his first trapping in the Adirondacks here.

The second line went up the Boreas River to the dam. Then the line went on to the Boreas River Ponds and east to Boreas Mountain. Then back to Wolf Pond Creek to Wolf Pond and back to camp.

The third line went down Boreas River to Cherry Pond. The line went around Cherry Pond and down to the dam then continued down the Boreas River. It continued to Vanderwhacker's Brook where the line went up the brook and across to Cherry Pond. It finished by going up the Boreas River to camp.

Dick noted that Trout Creek was true to its name as it teemed with trout. He vowed to come back and fish it. He came back with Bill in August of 1919 to do just that. That fishing trip was very important as it was when Dick was first exposed to the idea of trapping the Cold River area by Bill.

Powell's house visited at a different time of the year.

On December 26, 1917, Dick married Beulah Graham in Daisy, Tennessee. At the time, Dick was residing in Oneida and Beulah in North Chattanooga. On December 27, they visited the Powell's and other old friends in Hixson. On December 28, Dick and Beulah stayed in room 304 at the Patton Hotel in Chattanooga. Beulah went to say goodbye to her parents and visit her sister.

Dick and Beulah departed for Hiltons, Virginia early in the morning on December 29. They took a taxi to the train terminal and arrived in Bristol, Virginia in the early afternoon. They ate at Everett's Restaurant and arrived at Hiltons that evening.

Photographs of this grey fox were used in a Triumph Trap Company advertisement in the October 1919 issue of the National Sportsman. The photographs were used in several other Triumph advertisements.

On January 2, 1918, Dick was able to get some fox photos at his Uncle Gaines' farm to use in Triumph literature. The photograph of the grey fox would be used in numerous Triumph Trap Company advertisements and brochures. They also visited his Aunt Molly's farm and took more pictures off the Orchard Hill.

On January 3, Dick and Beulah went to Bristol to shop. In the evening on January 4, they arrived in New York City. On January 5, Dick called for and received a $50 check from Oneida at the Manhattan Hotel. They spent most of the day shopping at R. H. Macys and a few other shops. While in New York City, Dick and Beulah visited Belden and Milton Schreiber.

On January 6, Dick and Beulah took a taxi to Grand Central Station enroute back to Oneida. They arrived back in Oneida on January 7.

On January 8, Dick returned to his job at the Triumph Trap Factory. He worked on routine office tasks. He noted he was keeping banking hours.

Dick's trapping partner, Bill Wood.

On January 14, Dick was at Bill Wood's cabin at Racquette Lake. During this trip, he heard a beaver gnawing on a log under the ice. Dick scraped the snow away and shot at it without success. They set several beaver, otter and fisher traps. In Dick's May 1919 Fur News article titled "A Trapper's Musings, No. VIII – The Victory Dance", Dick used an alias of Bill DuBois for Bill Wood. He used this alias because "bois" is the French word for wood.

February 4 was a Government holiday, so Dick, Beulah and Beulah's friend, who was nicknamed "Doc", went skiing. It started to snow too hard to enjoy being outside so they went home. They stayed in the house the rest of the day on the floor around the oil stove telling stories.

On February 6, Dick commented that he got into work at 9:15 am and was still keeping banking hours. He said he expected to turn a new leaf in the morning.

Dick did turn a new leaf as he headed for Big Moose Lake in the Adirondacks. He arrived in zero degree weather with five feet of snow on the ground. Dick made the acquaintance of a French-Canadian trapper named Robert Wall. Robert agreed to trap with Dick using Dick's equipment except he would provide his own gun and snowshoes.

Bill Wood in a cabin.

Dick had two weeks of provisions and intended to stay in the woods for that amount of time. They loaded a toboggan and started in the general direction of the Sisters Lakes. Later they trapped down the Moose River to the south

Dick setting traps on the Moose River while at Big Moose Lake in 1918. This photograph was used on the cover of the April 1922 issue of Fur News and Outdoor World, the December 1934 issue of Fur Fish Game and the 1935-1936 issue of Hill Brothers Fur Company Catalog. The negative was flipped on the Fur Fish Game and Hill Brothers cover to produce a photograph where he is facing the other direction.

of Big Moose station travelling to Minnehaha and then took the train back. They looked for fisher, fox, mink, and bobcat.

In the fall, Robert had constructed a hunting camp on the shore of a small pond near Sisters Lakes. Dick commented that there was no wood in camp except for him, but he was too green to burn. The next day, they cut two weeks of wood.

Robert set out a line of traps around the Sisters Lakes for fox and mink. Weasel tracks were everywhere and they caught a dozen around their camp. Dick even shot one feeding on discarded table scraps. Dick put a line around camp and through a swamp for weasel and mink.

For bait, Robert caught suckers through the ice on the pond and rabbits caught in the traps. Once they had enough bait, Dick and Robert made an overnight trip. Both started for Big Moose and took the train south until they arrived at the Moose River flag station. They set traps as they travelled up the river and then went cross country back to camp.

There was plenty of beaver sign but they were protected. They had to be careful not to catch them in otter sets. There were a few springs that made excellent sets for mink. They also made two dozen sets for muskrat.

Dick and Robert left the Moose River at the mouth of the basin between two mountain ranges. They found several places for fisher sets. The trip took the better part of two days. They camped in a lean-to on a tributary of the Moose in a thick balsam swamp. This lean-to would be Dick's overnight camp. A couple of blankets, skillet, coffee pot and a few tallow candles were left there. Weasels were numerous between the Moose River and camp. Fifteen sets were made for them along the way.

The first trip over the line netted a couple of muskrats, a mink and several weasels. While checking, Dick had followed a fisher track back to a porcupine den. He went back over the line and pulled enough traps to secure the capture of that fisher. Dick commented that this was the first year that fisher pelts were quoted by reliable fur buyers at $100. This sum warranted considerable pains in trap setting.

Dick was out of bait but shot a snowshoe hare with his .22 Colt. The fisher's den was on a rock ledge where it had plenty of places to come out. Dick plastered the area with baited and blind sets. He reached the main camp an hour after dark.

The next day, Robert and Dick returned to the rock ledge, but none of the traps were disturbed. The third time over the line Dick caught a medium sized male fisher. The fisher was full of porcupine quills.

It started to rain and the trappers pulled their traps. They had to wait four days for it to freeze again so they could walk out.

On February 26 of 1918, Dick took a trip to Malone, New York, with Duane Joslin. Duane was a fur buyer from Cazenovia, New York. They took a trolley from Oneida to Utica and then a train to Boonville. Dick and Duane stayed at the Hubbert House. On February 27 while in Boonville, Duane bought $250 worth of fur including fox, mink, skunk and ermine.

From there, they took a train to Remsen where they stayed at the Bristol House. Remsen was a dry town. While waiting for the train to Tupper Lake, Dick read Field and Stream and wrote while Duane played Pitch with a bunch of lumberjacks. On February 28 after reaching Tupper Lake, Dick and Duane took pictures after walking a half mile over ice on the lake. That evening, they started for Malone.

Dick and Duane arrived in Malone on March 1. They stayed in the Smith House. Dick and Duane met with mink trapping expert Pat Mannis. Pat was a reputable fur buyer who had been in business over 20 years. Dick and Duane also stopped at the Malone Iron Rag and Hide Company. Due to Duane's persuasion, they left on a night train to Oneida. Pat had proposed a trip with Lute Trim which Duane thought was more interesting than travelling with Dick. They were back in Oneida on March 2.

On March 3, Dick developed the film from the trip and went to the Triumph Trap Factory with Beulah. They stayed at the office and talked to Frances E. Adams until 8:00 pm.

Dick is second from the left side. Frances E. Adams is the furthest on the right of the photo. Photo was taken in front of the Triumph Trap Factory in Oneida, New York.

On March 4, Dick was at the Triumph Trap Factory in the morning. That afternoon, he and Beulah went out to check some traps. Dick took pictures of a skunk they caught. He developed the film and skinned the skunk that night. He got home at 11:00 pm.

On March 7 of 1918, Dick started travelling to Maryland. He spent that night at the Wilmot Hotel in Philadelphia. On March 8, Dick continued traveling.

From March 9 to 15, Dick and Holdridge Greene, another Triumph employee, visited Walter A. Gibbs who was a trap manufacturer in Maryland. Gibbs had a large marsh filled with muskrats where he had developed the Two Trigger trap. The trap would catch each muskrat by the body as well as the foot. This trap eliminated the possibility of the muskrat escaping. The Triumph Trap Company explored the possibility of manufacturing the trap for Gibbs, but never did.

In his book "The Steel Trap in North America", Richard Gerstell comments that Dick had told Gerstell that he was the one who recommended that Triumph not manufacture the Two Trigger. Dick said that decision was his biggest mistake.

Dick wrote an article about trapping with Gibbs. The title was "Boots and Marshes" published in two parts in the May and June 1918 issues of Fur News. Although not as detailed as "Boots and Marshes", Dick wrote another article about this trip. The title was "Muskrat Trapping on Marshes" published in the June 1919 issue of Hunter Trader Trapper. Both articles included photographs taken at Gibbs' marsh.

Gibbs had five trappers catching fifty to one hundred muskrats each a day when Dick arrived. Dick, being a duck hunter at heart, commented that the marsh was a regular bird paradise. He took numerous photos of the marsh, muskrat huts and muskrats in the Two Trigger trap. He had a couple of miscues that included breaking his camera tripod and then losing it. Unfortunately, some of the film seemed to be light struck and other film had no appearance of being exposed. Dick made prints from some good negatives and shared those with Gibbs.

Gibbs had sent Dick letters inviting him down to help trap muskrats. Gibbs always included a reminder to not forget his rubber boots at the end of the letters. Dick arrived in the village and was met by Gibbs. Gibbs took him to the hotel to eat and discuss their trapping plans. Gibbs asked if Dick had brought his boots and Dick responded that he had. Gibbs wanted to look them over to make sure they were quality boots. Dick assured him that the boots were the best he could get. They departed the town without looking at them. The village was the only place where boots could be purchased in the area.

Dick and Gibbs loaded into a mud-boat vehicle. They took a 12 mile journey on a mud road which turned into a corduroy road. They drove through an iron gate into the compound. All the walks and driveways inside the compound were corduroyed with poles and planks. The compound had a house with a wide veranda, a bunk house, a garage and a workshop with a curing room. Hundreds of muskrat pelts were already hung in the curing room.

For supper, they had roast duck, marsh rabbit, oysters from the

This photograph was also taken when Dick trapped with Gibbs. It was used in many Triumph Trap Company brochures.

Chesapeake, Maryland apples, jellies, pies and many other items that quickly subdued their appetites. After spending some time on the veranda listening to the noises of the marsh, they headed off to bed.

After breakfast the next morning, Gibbs suggested looking over the gear that Dick had brought before heading out to trap. Dick opened his duffle bag to find his 16 inch boots instead of his hip waders. Dick commented that they were packed by another member of the family while Dick attended to other details of preparing for the trip.

Gibbs was disappointed in this and accurately guessed that there was not another pair of hip waders at his place that would fit Dick. Dick told Gibbs that the boots he had were water proof and lighter than waders, so he would be fine.

Gibbs sold live muskrats and the following series of photographs shows the technique used to capture them.

47

The traps had to be set so the captured muskrat would not be held under water and drown.

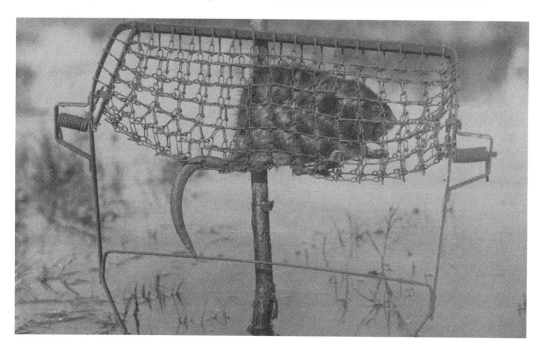

Cans with lids were used to transport the muskrats after capture.

Dick and five other trappers started out to the marsh. They left the fenced in lot and followed the main bank until they met a cross ditch. Each trapper had their own line of one to two hundred traps. Two trappers went to the left and two went to the right. Dick followed Gibbs on his line which circled the center of the marsh.

As Dick stepped off the ditch bank, he tried to land on a high spot and he did until he took another step on a bunch of swamp grass that wobbled and let him down into the quagmire up to his knees. The harder he struggled, the deeper he sank. Dick looked up to Gibbs for help just as Gibbs took off to recover a muskrat he saw struggling in a trap. Dick struggled out of the mess and climbed back on top of solid ground. His new technique was to jump between high spots.

Skinning at Gibbs' building. Two photos, which are similar to this one, were used in the June 1918 issue of Fur News and the June 1919 issue of Hunter Trader Trapper.

Dick and Gibbs had made considerable progress and caught two dozen muskrats. They completed the circle and started for the house. They arrived back at the house, but not before the other four trappers. The six trappers caught ninety-one muskrats. The other trappers spent the rest of the day skinning the muskrats and boarding the ones caught the previous day.

Dick realized, the hard way, hip waders were a necessity for marsh travelling. He sauntered around the place looking for a solution to his dilemma. There were boats around, but the marsh was too shallow to use them.

Dick returned to the skinning room and happened to find a pair of canvas overalls and a can of boiled linseed oil. The ends of the legs were sown together. Dick soaked the legs in a solution containing linseed oil, alum and rosin. He then hung them up overnight to dry. The next morning, the legs were dried and completely waterproof. Dick put them on and pulled a pair of boots over the top of them.

Gibbs had been picking up some of his traps to get down to a minimum number for trapping the remaining few days of the season. Dick had out less than two dozen. Both of their lines were short and they were the first ones to get in, on most days.

Several poles were placed throughout the marsh. Gibbs attached traps to the tops of these poles to catch hawks, owls and eagles. He called them his "camouflage" traps. These birds made quite an impact on the muskrat population and would take trapped muskrats, trap and all. Gibbs worked hard to keep the population of these birds down so that the muskrat population would not be impacted.

On March 12, Dick stayed up until 11:00 pm playing cards with Fanny Elsey, Gibbs' bookkeeper. Before they quit playing, Gibbs came down to see how things were moving along.

There were two days left in the season and a front was about to work through the area. The next day all six trappers set out as many traps as they could. It rained the following day and the marsh was six inches higher than the day before. The six trappers caught three hundred twenty-nine muskrats, well over the usual daily average. The marsh usually produced two to four thousand rats a year and the trappers would average a total catch of one hundred each day. The muskrat season in Dorchester County ended on March 15.

Dick left for Oneida after checking the traps one last time. He sent a $6 box of cigars back for Gibbs and a box of candy for Fanny. Dick ate at Ostendorff's in Philadelphia and arrived in New York City at midnight.

Dick had one very interesting comment about his visit. He said that a still and gin mill were running full fledge.

Predatory bird caught in a Gibbs Hawk trap.

On his way back to Oneida, Dick stopped at Racquette Lake to help Bill Wood snowshoe in to Pelcher Lake to get Bill's cached furs. They utilized a toboggan to get the furs out.

At lunch time, Dick and Bill stopped to eat. Bill built a brush lean-to to serve as a wind break. He cut green poles four feet long and laid those down on top of the snow as a base. Bill used the tops as the wall toward the wind. Bacon and flapjacks provided fuel for the remaining two miles.

Bill Wood built this lean-to where they ate on the way to get Bill's cached furs. This photograph was used on the cover of the December 1923 issue of Fur News and Outdoor World and the September 1936 issue of Fur Fish Game.

Bill never cashed his furs together. So when they arrived, Bill removed bundles of furs sewn in burlap from a large hollow pine tree, a hollow log and a rock ledge, all within one hundred twenty yards of each other. The toboggan was much heavier on the way out so both men hooked onto the harness to pull.

Dick and Bill had broken trail as they traveled in, but snow started to fall on their way out. After six inches had fallen, they took turns breaking the trail while the other one pulled the heavy toboggan. The storm was now at blizzard strength with the day ending.

Dick on frozen Racquette Lake. This photograph was used in the editorial article titled "Dick Wood has hit the Trail and Trap Line again" in the September 1922 issue of Fur News and Outdoor World.

At first, they traded positions every half mile. By the time they reached the ice of Racquette Lake, they were trading every hundred yards. Dick and Bill kept in constant communication with each other to make sure neither got hurt or disoriented. It was dark once they reached Racquette Lake and Bill used a compass to lead them to his cabin in town.

Dick in front of the Triumph Trap Company factory.

From March 26 through 30, Dick worked at his office at the Triumph Trap Company. On April 1 of 1918, Dick met with Robert Wall again to get pictures for an article about their trap line at Big Moose Lake. Robert got on the train at Fulton Chain with a bunch of lumberjacks. He was drunk so Dick proceeded to Big Moose and stayed with a French Canadian by the name of Will Jarvis who ran a boarding house. Will acted as a guide for Dick the next day. Dick took some pictures of trapping, camping and scenery. The next morning, he worked on the pictures and then left on a train back to Oneida. Dick was back at his office in the Triumph Trap Factory at noon on April 4. On April 5, Dick and Joslin took a trip to Rome in the afternoon.

On April 8, Dick left on another trip. He spent the night in Hormell at the York Hotel. The next day he met F. E. Brimmer at his home in Dalton. Brimmer was a principal at a local high school. Dick spent the day with him. After eating supper, Dick left for Binghamton by way of Hornell. He stayed in the Arlington Hotel that night.

Dick used a few of F.E. Brimmer's drawings in his articles. This drawing was used in the article titled "Trapping the Mink" in the October 12, 1918 issue of The Nebraska Farmer.

F. E. Brimmer wrote about his meeting with Dick in his article titled "By-Products of the Trap Line" in the August 1918 issue of Fur News. Brimmer called Dick a "live-wire" trapper. He liked Dick because he was an idealist and always moved under the inspiration of planning bigger and better things for the future. Dick was not satisfied to do this year no better than he did last, but visualized more efficient trap setting, more carefully planned trap lines, and greater catches.

Dick and Brimmer agreed setting traps is not all of trapping. The by-products of the trap line constitute the greater part of the fascination of trapping. Somehow the toil and hardships of the backwoods completely vanish and only the surprises, the thrills, the exciting escapes, the clever outwitting of a fox, the

F.E. Brimmer with a bobcat.

glamour of achievement, and the joy of living close to nature with her never ending wonders.

On April 10, Dick stopped at the Ansco Company and met Mr. Field who was their Advertising Manager. They exchanged ideas on advertising pictures and in an hour Dick left with a present of one dozen films for only Ansco Speedex film cameras. He arrived back in Oneida on April 11.

This photograph of Dick in Michigan was used in advertising for Corona typewriters.

On April 15, Dick left for Ogdensburg to meet with E.J. Dailey. Beulah accompanied him to Syracuse where Dick spent $32.50 on spring clothes for her. Beulah returned to Oneida and Dick continued to Ogdensburg. After arriving, Dick went to the Ogdensburg Hotel and wrote several business letters on his Corona.

The next day, E.J. picked him up at the hotel in his Ford. This was the first season that E.J. was using an automobile to run his traps. Before this, E.J. had walked or more recently used a horse. They checked traps in the afternoon and caught nine muskrats. The next day the trap line produced ten muskrats. E.J. had about two hundred traps out and averaged ten to twenty-five muskrats a day. He was only using blind sets.

It stormed that night. The next day was cold with high winds and snow. E.J. and Dick did not go out to check the traps. Dick wrote, listened to banjo music and made twelve plates for his camera. The muskrat season in New York in 1918 closed on April 20, so they pulled traps.

On May 27, Dick started on his first sales trip. His trip started at Norwich, New York, and continued southward into Pennsylvania. He sold his first fifty-two dozen traps in Norwich. He then went through Oxford and stayed in Guilford.

On the second day, Dick traveled through Sidney, Bainbridge and Afton selling another eight dozen traps. On the third day, he traveled through Windsor and Handcock. Dick sold another forty-four dozen traps. The last day of the trip, he did not have any luck selling as it was the Decoration Day holiday.

In the fall of 1918, Dick trapped with Bill Wood from Racquette Lake. They used a camp south of Haymarsh ponds and north of Sucker Brook, Shallow Lake and Pelsher Lake. This area was located northwest of Racquette Lake.

The fur prices were excellent with skunk at $7.50, muskrats at $1, mink at $9 and fox at $30. In the month of November, Dick and Bill covered twenty miles a day and trapped marshes, deep woods and clearings. They focused on skunk, muskrats and fox.

By the end of November, Dick and Bill had taken the traps at water sets and transferred them to cubbies in tall timber for fisher and marten. On November 26, Dick caught a fisher in a hollow tree and shot a buck. On November 27, Dick and Bill set fisher traps. Dick was setting a fisher trap when a red fox came down a hillside. He shot it with a 45-70.

On December 1, Dick commented he walked at least six miles through fifteen inches of freshly fallen snow. He was fisher trap setting, deer looking and picture taking. At Bill Wood's cabin, Dick noted he had plenty of pets including five whiskey jacks, two chickadees, one weasel and numerous mice.

In early February of 1919, Dick and Bill took their canoe down the swift Sucker Brook. It was narrow, but deep enough to qualify as a river. They pulled mink sets along the way. They reached still water caused by a beaver dam a quarter mile further down the brook. The still water had ice thick enough to walk on.

In October of 1918, Inez, Dick's daughter, was born in Oneida. This photograph of Beulah and baby carriage holding Inez was taken in Central Park in Oneida on April 4 of 1919.

Dick and Bill caught a mink at the beaver dam and set a trap for an otter that had crossed over the dam. From the beaver dam, they went north to Duck Pond and then followed another brook south to their camp. They made fisher, marten and otter sets along this line.

Shortly after this venture, Dick and Bill decided to part ways for the winter. Dick headed back to the Holston River in Virginia. He arrived in Hiltons and went to the combination hotel, grocery-hardware-dry goods store, notary public and sheriff's hangout. Dick asked if anyone was trapping his old stomping grounds. A few men stepped forward to greet him. They told him that the local trappers had pulled their traps because it had been too cold to tend them.

Trappers starting out for the day on Racquette Lake. This photograph was used on the cover of the April 1923 issue of Fur News and Outdoor World.

Bill Wood making an otter set on a beaver dam. This photograph was used in the article titled "Beaver Trapping – Past and Present" in the February 1924 issue of Fur News and Outdoor World.

The family boat on the North Fork of the Holston River below Dick's mother's house. This photograph was used in Triumph literature.

Even with the previous competition, Dick wanted to check the river out to see what was still there. He got the family's skiff and drifted down the river scouting for fur sign. He drifted in short sleeves but had seen others in full outdoor gear. The time in the Adirondacks had acclimatized him to colder temperatures.

Lute Trim, in the doorway, with another trapper.

Dick saw plenty of fresh sign. The sign and ideal outdoor weather induced him to retrieve a bunch of rusty traps he had hung in the smokehouse before he left in 1917. Dick worked on the traps to make sure they were strong enough to hold the animals he was after. Dick recommended using opossum grease or fish oil to lubricate traps and increase the trapper's success. He said these were much better than axle grease, machine oil or other foreign smelling preparations. Dick caught raccoon, opossum, skunk and muskrats on this line.

Dick shot a rabbit with his .22 while sitting under an evergreen tree when visiting Lute Trim.

Dick met Lute Trim in early 1919. Dick took a mail stage coach for twenty miles south of Malone to Lute's house by Duane, New York. They checked Lute's traps. Dick said he hit the wrong season and did not see many furs taken except for numerous fox. There was an undue scarcity of furbearers near Lute's area. An indication of the quality of trapper Lute was. Dick said that Lute could make sets in the snow for fox and produce results immediately.

For thirty-eight years, Lute guided for Governor Lounsbury of Connecticut, first at Meacham and later Racquette Lake. Lute was the supervisor of the Town of Duane and the vice-president of the Malone Fish and Game Club.

In Dick's book titled "Trapping as a Profession", Dick commented Lute caught a wolf the next season. There was some controversy about this wolf capture. It was said to have been captured on January 20, 1920. The pelt was exhibited in Malone to support the story that Lute Trim had caught a genuine timber wolf in a trap on Duane Mountain and it was one of a pack. This created a sensation throughout the Adirondacks.

The New York State Conservation Commission sent Inspector Byron Cameron of Saranac Lake to investigate. After Inspector Cameron's investigation, the Conservation Commission announced the wolf story was a hoax. The pelt was from a timber wolf, but it had been sent to Lute from someone out west.

In late February of 1919, Dick ventured to trap on the Wicomico River which flows into the Chesapeake Bay in Maryland. He took a passenger boat of the same name as the river to get there. Upon arrival, he was held at gun point until his identity could be ascertained.

While waiting, Dick reflected on his predicament. He remembered being shot at when he approached too close to hidden moonshine stills in the Cumberlands. He was held up once in Nashville, Tennessee, and while fishing from a schooner in the Gulf of Mexico, he was thrown overboard. This was the first time he had been taken prisoner for no good reason.

Dick had not let the Manning brothers, Sam and Calvin, know he was coming. The Manning brothers were extensive muskrat trappers. After a few hours of talking about trapping, everything was smoothed over.

Dick trapped the Wicomico River marches with the Manning brothers until heavy rain made the water deeper than could be trapped. The water stayed high for over a week. Every day lost meant less money and one day closer to the end of season. The brothers planned a shooting trip to make up for the loss in trapping catches even though shooting muskrats was illegal.

They were about to set their plans in motion when they noticed a light on the marsh and then heard gun fire. Someone had beaten them to the punch. Dick

Moonshiners by Silver Springs, Florida. Definitely not the ones that shot at Dick.

and the two brothers traveled out on the marsh in a boat. The brothers loaded their pockets with 12-gauge shotgun shells. Dick decided he did not want to carry a firearm.

They let Sam off and he proceeded along a trail on the bank with the goal of getting behind the shooters. Dick and Calvin continued to paddle quietly toward the shooters. Soon Calvin identified the shooters by their voices. He said it was the Laneys and that they sounded intoxicated. Thorp Laney had sworn to shoot Sam the next time he saw him.

Sam was carrying a double barrel shotgun. He fired both barrels at the same time which resulted in the shooters putting out the light. They continued to yell and cuss which resulted in another double shot. At this point, the shooters were quiet except for the noise they made swimming to the opposite shore.

One of Sam's shots made a large hole in their boat which caused it to sink. Dick put their light on the sunken boat and found about sixty dead muskrats.

Trapping and illegal shooting had decreased the muskrat populations to the point that the brothers did not want to trap their area any longer. They had already taken 1,400 rats. Sam and Dick decided to rent a 300 acre marsh further up the river. They trapped it for the next month.

The catch was dwindling and Dick decided it was time to move on. The Manning brothers pointed out that he could not leave the area until he visited the

Kinney brothers. They were the most famous trappers on the Wicomico River. Dick found that Jim and Ed Kinney were the best trappers on the Wicomico and had the best trapping section in the area. After the muskrat season ended in Maryland, Dick returned to New York State to trap spring muskrats with E.J. Dailey.

This photograph is from a Triumph advertisement in the February and March 1919 editions of the Hunter Trader Trapper.

Dick had been so busy with his many trapping excursions, he made a mistake on a Triple Clutch advertisement in the February and March 1919 issues of Hunter Trader Trapper. The advertisement shows two photographs. One was of a fisher caught in a 2-X double long spring. The other was titled "His Pelt", but the pelt was of a weasel. In the April edition, a different Triple Clutch advertisement was posted. This notes the error and states "Our Advertising Dept. has promised "Dick" Wood to be more careful in the future."

Fishermen on the Boreas River.

In August of 1919, Dick fished the Boreas River for Trout with Bill Randall. This was a very important fishing trip because Dick was exposed to the idea of trapping the Cold River area by Bill. He had been there twenty years before while working as a log driver. Bill told Dick he had caught several dozen fox one winter in one or two traps set out back of the camp. Dick investigated it further and convinced E.J. Dailey to make a trip there scouting for fur.

Bill was glad to see Dick and the new fox trap he had brought him. They drove the 40 miles back to the river spot. The road was mostly uphill causing the vehicle to overheat a couple of times.

Beavers had dammed a tributary off the Boreas and created a pond full of trout. Bill had previously stashed a boat at the pond. They climbed in the boat and started fishing. Bill got bites quicker than Dick because he went with a simple rig of a hook with worms while Dick tried to tie up flies. Bill would catch a fish and swing the fish toward the opposite end of the boat for Dick to unhook it. This hindered Dick from catching very many. Finally, he did and they were happy with the number of fish they had so they stopped to clean them.

During the week of trout fishing, they had been eating trout twice a day. Dick and Bill needed a little variety in their food. They were trout fishing when it started to rain. The rain facilitated the biting of bullheads. They continued to fish in the rain and soon had a basket full. They arrived at camp a few hours later and cleaned the fish. They ate the bullheads as if they were a new dish to them.

Dick and Bill fished a couple more days and then drove to the Village of Schroon Lake to take in the movies and visit the ice cream parlors. Dick called a Ford car the connecting link between civilization and the wilderness. The next day, they traveled up to Wolf Pond. This pond was where Dick did his first trapping in the Adirondacks.

Bill passed away during the winter of 1925-1926. Dick wrote three different articles for three different magazines about his passing showing he was on Dick's mind and had influenced him.

In late October of 1919, Dick and E.J. Dailey explored the Cold River country of the Adirondacks. They took a train to Lake Placid and got a truck ride southward as far as the road would go. They then walked the rest of the way in. Many of Dick's later articles, about camping and hiking, mentioned his pack on this trip weighed 80 pounds and his .303 Savage weighed 8 pounds. He learned through time his pack should have weighed less than half this weight and he should have carried a lighter rifle.

Dick called the Cold River trail a gift from the Santa Clara Lumber Company that had worked in the area. The trail provided an easy transportation route along the river where the water was too swift to freeze. Dick used the

E.J. at Duck Hole in the Cold River area.

frozen river surface as a transportation route where it was calm enough to freeze.

Dick and E.J. were equipped for three weeks and could extend their stay with game they harvested along the way. The first night they camped at Moose Pond. The next day, they traveled south into the heart of the Adirondacks. There was no trail and the going was very tough. They were preoccupied with the weight on their backs and not prepared for the bear that jumped from the shelter of a large leaning snag. The bear was gone before they could get to their guns. Dick kept his rifle ready the rest of the day. That night, they camped at the edge of a little stream and ate two grouse E.J. shot with his shotgun.

Early the next day, it looked like rain, but they did not set up camp before the rain hit. Dick and E.J. hastily set up camp in the rain. It rained all night and was rather cold in the tent. E.J. commented that his equipment for an outing was usually a frying pan, a hunting knife and a rifle. He found the alcohol stove and two very small charcoal stoves that Dick brought were very welcomed.

The next day they entered a stretch of country that had been lumbered in the past. It made walking a little easier. Deer were plentiful here based on tracks and observations. That night they found an unlocked log cabin by the headwaters of Cold River.

Cabin at Duck Hole in the Cold River area.

Dick and E.J. walked inside and dropped their heavy packs on the floor. The cabin had a box style stove, a table with dishes on it and two bunks built into the wall. They stayed the night.

Dick and E.J. were hungry for fresh meat after eating bacon everyday. They decided to fish for trout in Cold River. They sat down on a log to figure out what to use for bait. E.J. suggested a piece of bacon. Dick, absent mindedly, began stripping off pieces of dead bark from the log and exposed several fat grubs. They both went to work on the log with knives and a belt axe. Soon they had a can full of wood borers and caught a fine mess of fish.

73

E.J. on his trap line away from Cold River.

The next day they saw a dilapidated dam across the stream. The cabin had been used by a dam keeper who worked for the lumber company. They found an old road and realized there was probably an easier way in than they had come. This road would be a great help. It would have been impossible to get a winter's supply of food and three hundred traps to their camp by the route they had just travelled.

Dick and E.J. followed the road to where it branched. Then they followed the branch of the road along the river. At sunset, they found another cabin. There was evidence of another dam which had been washed out. This cabin was not in as good of condition as the first. This cabin would later be used by Dick as an overnight cabin.

The next day they headed back to the first cabin. On the way, they hunted. Dick shot a deer. Dick and E.J. spent over a week scouting the area around the cabin.

They found plenty of furbearer sign and were satisfied they accomplished what they wanted. They took the old road and found a lumber camp where they got a ride out to Tupper Lake. A French Canadian was the boss at the lumber camp. After talking to him, he said that they could ship him their traps, and he would keep them until they came back to trap.

In the fall of 1919, Dick trapped with E.J. on his St. Lawrence trap line. They both used E.J.'s traps as Dick's traps had been transported to the lumber camp. They were catching ten skunks, a dozen muskrats and a coon or mink a day. The catch was too good for them to head back to the Cold River area as early as they had expected.

E.J.'s line ran along the St. Lawrence River for about fifty miles and turned at Beaver Creek. Skunk was mainly targeted in this area. The line then headed toward Lone Lake, good mink territory, and proceeded to the featherbed ridges where fox and skunk were plentiful. The line then headed to Crooked Creek where muskrats were plentiful. From there it worked along the Grass River and then to Highy's Flats, a marshy muskrat section. It then drifted along the Adirondack foothills in the southern part of St. Lawrence County.

After Christmas of 1919, Dick, E.J. and Bill Wood returned to the Cold River country of the Adirondacks. They stopped at the local lumber company and found a team was heading back to the camp the next day. They got written permission to use the dam keeper's cabin at Cold River from the Santa Clara Lumber Company.

After they arrived at the lumber camp, they had to transverse the remaining six miles by foot. There was five feet of snow and they had two hundred pounds on a toboggan, three loaded packs and three rifles. To say the going was challenging was an understatement.

On the way to the cabin at Duck Hole. This photograph is very similar to the one used on the cover of the January 1923 issue of Fur News and Outdoor World except the person closest to the camera is carrying a box of tomato soup on his left shoulder instead of traps.

Dick taking a lunch break on the Cold River trail. The Heinz box referenced in the caption of the previous photograph is in this photograph. He may have tried to sell this photograph to that company.

Bill Wood at Dick's line cabin with a fisher pelt and a Triumph trap

Dick, E.J. and Bill arrived at the cabin that evening. The next day they put things in order, caught a few fish through the ice and cut a supply of fire wood.

After supper, they flipped a coin to find out where Dick and E.J. would trap. Dick won and chose the section extending down Cold River to the lower dam, then to Mountain Pond and back by the way of Panther Peak and Otter Creek.

E.J. chose the line down the road to Moose Pond, then to Slow Brook and through a notch in the Sawtooth Range to Roaring Brook. He would come around Rock Ponds and follow Cold River back to the cabin. Both lines were two day trips. E.J. would have to build an overnight shelter and Dick would use the cabin at the lower dam.

Bill ran a weasel line around the cabin and did the cooking. He would hunt for fresh game, such as rabbit, as well.

A period of poor weather put Dick, E.J. and Bill in the cabin together for a month. This extended stay in close quarters made Dick notice EJ's weakness for shaving. Being away from civilization, Dick let his facial hair grow and did not understand why E.J. shaved each day. E.J. said it provided him a great deal of satisfaction in doing so.

Dick had a weakness for French literature. He read the Bible, Pilgrim's Progress, Dante's Inferno and others when away from civilization. As Dick read Balzac each night, E.J. snuffed out the candle with his six shooter. One night Dick had had enough of this, so he emptied his automatic Colt into the wall over E.J.'s head. That stopped the candle business.

E.J. left when it started snowing everyday and his snowshoes had worn out. He made a pair from barrel hoops and telephone wire so he could leave the Cold River area. Bill went with him. Dick stayed alone for several weeks. The only other people in the area with him were lumberjacks who were six miles away.

Dick made a point of passing around the lumber camp boss' favorite brand of stogies on his periodical visits to the camp. Dick wanted to stay on his good side to make sure that his mail was brought out regularly as well as any supplies he requested.

Almost every time Dick would run his Cold River line near the steep ranges, he would see huge snow slides rushing down the steep mountains. They would leave destruction in their wake and a cloud of fine snow in the air.

Where the line ran along Panther Peak, the walking was extremely rough. Fisher were moving around this area a great deal and, since they were worth $100 that year, Dick was expanding considerable time and energy to catch as many as he could. Because the snow was so deep, Dick had to be very careful tending marten traps set in higher altitudes. If he fell, Dick could have started an avalanche or sprained an ankle. Either incident would be disastrous because he was so far from any help.

Dick had another line extending down river that took two days to tend. He also had a loop around Duck Hole.

Bill Wood setting a trap. Photograph was used on the cover of the March 1922 issue of Fur News and Outdoor World.

Pulling the toboggan.

Starting out on the Cold River trail.

The day that E.J. and Bill left, Dick loaded his packsack with his sleeping bag, a few traps and headed out for two days. Dick said he was a solitude loving guy, but he wanted to keep busy in the sudden absence of his partners. He did not want a chance to take on the blues.

Dick setting a trap under a tote road bridge.

Dick found a weasel in the first trap he checked. The trap was under a tote road bridge. He had traps around the outlet of a small lake. He missed an otter, but caught a couple of muskrats. Dick continued down a brook and was amazed at the number of deer wintering in the narrow valley.

Dick picked up a few traps to move to Cold River. He saw a dark object flashing across the snow not more than twenty feet ahead. A young buck was floundering through a deer trail. Dick intercepted the deer and it veered off the trail into deep soft snow where it sank up to its belly. Dick got close to the deer with his snowshoes and took some close-up photographs.

The buck was extremely thin and in a weakened condition from lack of food. Dick made sure he did not get too close out of respect of its sharp hooves. When alone in the woods far from civilization, he shunned close encounters with wild animals and watched his step with guns, thin ice, rock bluffs, and other dangers.

At a cubby pen set on a wooded knoll in the Cold River valley, Dick caught a marten. From this point down river to Dick's line camp, traps were scattered and he spent a short afternoon setting fox traps. It was dark when he arrived at his line cabin and had to cook by candle light.

The return route back to the main cabin followed tote roads through the woods most of the way. All the sets were for land animals. Dick also had a loop around a mountain peak for martin. He took a couple weasels from traps set in hollow logs and snags. It was an exceedingly hard two days back to Duck Hole.

The next traps that Dick checked were around Mountain Pond, a small lake located at high elevation. He stayed the night at Camp One.

When Dick arrived at Camp One, he found that the last person had taken the stove pipe. He fashioned one out of tar paper but its use resulted in nearly burning the cabin down. Dick used his "Comfort Sleeping Pocket". He could sleep as warm as toast in a place as open as a barn. The trip back to the main cabin only took a half a day, so the rest of the day was used to thaw out the animals and skin them.

The line to Panther Peak followed a brook and most of the traps up the mountain were set for mink. The line then looped back to Preston Ponds.

Dick ran short on food shortly before he left the Cold River trap line. He cut a hole through the ice on Henderson Lake to fish for trout. He used a chunk of bacon for bait and caught several nice trout. He used some of the trout for bait and caught a mink at the lake.

Dick at his line cabin.

This photograph was used on the cover of the February 1921 issue of Fur News and Outdoor World.

After a month of fair trapping weather, warming temperatures started to melt the snow. Dick was caught at his line cabin in a warm rain and had two tough days getting out of the area. Dick did not have a food supply at the camp.

He was carrying a forty pound pack sinking six inches into the soft snow and lifting five pounds of snow with each step.

Dick was exhausted when he reached Camp One without any food. He decided to try to make the lumber camp by crossing through a gap in the mountains. Dick estimated it was a four mile trip. He cached the traps at Camp One. Dick thought himself a fool for not having a barometer in camp to track the weather.

An hour after dark, Dick reached his toboggan trail between the main cabin and the lumber camp. The lumber camp was closer than the main cabin, so he cached his pack and headed for the prospect of cooked food. After dark, the snow on the toboggan trail started to freeze making the traveling easier.

Dick made it to the lumber camp and cooked food. He slept on an improvised bed in the office building and was up at 4:00 am the next morning. Dick managed to toboggan his furs and personal duffel down to the lumber camp by working at night when the trail was frozen.

A few days after getting his possessions out, a pole bridge was washed out by a stream swollen with melting snow. It would have stranded him at a camp without food for two weeks during a season when, according to Dick, hunting and fishing were almost fruitless.

Dick said he caught seventeen mink from one spot while on the Cold River line. The mink were caught under the debris of an old building that was almost entirely covered with snow. The building had been a small barn within fifteen feet of the river just below a dam. Every mink that went up or down the river nosed around that area. The debris was held three feet above the ground and Dick had to crawl under it to set the trap. He nailed bait to one of the supports, rubbed some lure on it, and set a good Newhouse in the dry chaff below the bait. The set was always dry and the trap never froze or got covered by snow. It was an ideal set that worked regardless of the weather conditions.

Dick wrote about catching the seventeen mink in January 1926. He was no longer working for the Triumph Trap Company when he wrote the article but was when he trapped the mink. I wonder how he would have written the story if he still worked for Triumph when he wrote the article. Would the part about the Newhouse trap still be included?

After leaving the Cold River trap line, Dick returned to St. Lawrence County to trap with E.J. The season opened on March 20 in 1920. On April 8, Dick commented that the smaller creeks had frozen over the last three nights and hardly thawed during the day. Every body of water on this day was ice covered. The line produced only a couple of muskrats. He thought it should have produced a dozen. A blizzard raged all day and forced Dick to seek the shelter of a hay stack. It snowed several inches and he wondered how the folks were on the old Virginia farm.

E.J. setting a trap in a spring for mink.

Getting ready to take the furs out from the cabin at Duck Hole.

As soon as the ice went out, every muskrat trapper set out his traps. Competition was high due to the high price of fur. The amount of competition was much more than Dick had experienced at Cold River. The number of traps and how closely trappers set to each other was new to Dick, but E.J. informed him that that was the way it was and to start doing likewise.

Dick learned two important things which was the difference between a few rats and a whole lot of rats. First, most of the trappers were farmer's sons and they mostly wore Storm King or another low boot. Dick had a boot three inches higher allowing him to get to deeper runs where the farm boys could not without getting wet.

Second was a setting technique that E.J. had shown him. Other trappers set their traps at the underwater mouths of muskrat burrows. E.J. took a shovel and removed a chunk of sod down to the burrow above the mouth toward the bank. He would set his trap and stake it in the burrow so a muskrat with a trap and chain could not reach the mouth. Then he would put the chunk of sod carefully back in the hole from where it was cut.

The muskrat got caught coming out of the den and drown in the burrow. The other trappers did not know why they were not catching any muskrats. They could not see the drowned muskrat up in the burrow.

On one occasion, Dick had set a trap at one of two bank holes close together. He picked the one that had cloudy water. The next day he found the trap set, but in the other hole. Someone had been nice enough to reset the trap after taking Dick's muskrat, but did not put it in the same hole. E.J. found the spot where the person had climbed out on the bank and skinned the muskrat.

Dick and E.J. set traps around a pond and returned the next day to find a cheaper brand of trap in their place. They called it a season and pulled traps. They pulled the same amount they had set, but could not definitely say all the traps were ones they had set.

In the fall of 1920, Dick traveled to the Upper Peninsula of Michigan to trap with a person outside of Republic. The trapper had corresponded with Dick and convinced him to trap the area. The trapper controlled sixteen square miles of the Fence River area. Dick never said the name of this trapper, but had the opportunity to meet some quality trappers in the area including Dick Sutliff, Rolland Ames, Floyd Ames, Charlie Shellman and Frank Peterson.

On October 7, Dick left Oneida. He spent the next day in Chicago with Dan B. Starkey who was the editor of Outers Magazine and arrived in Republic on October 9. Dick was met by the trapper and his son. They shot some partridge on the ten minute drive to camp. On October 10, Dick hunted with the trapper's son, and they shot eleven partridge.

Dick found, instead of trapping, the trapper put him to work building a pond. A couple weeks of good weather were wasted doing this. The trapper kept making excuses for not setting traps, and Dick filled in the time outside of the tasks by hunting partridge.

Dick Sutliff of the wilderness west of Fence River on the Michigan Peninsula.

Dick at Sutliff's Cabin in northern Michigan. A photograph, very similar to this one, was used on the cover of the January 1933 issue of Fur Fish Game.

The tasks outside of trapping kept coming up. They included getting hay and storing it in the barn, repairing a road and making a sled. Dick felt like a hunter who was duped by a guide who charged him for a week to get the quarry

Dick Sutliff setting a trap for mink.

Dick making a set for bear using a 415X High Grip trap.

when it could have been gotten in a day. He decided to make it into a learning experience. Finally, on October 27, they set traps for bear, bobcat and mink. Dick also shot a spike horn buck.

On October 30, Dick shot two partridge with his .22. One was at 15 yards and the other was at 24 yards. The trapper set out more mink traps and caught the first one of the season on November 4. On November 13, Dick was photographing a weasel by camp when he noticed a 10 to 12-point buck scrapping his antlers on a bush 100 feet away. Dick tried unsuccessfully to sneak back to the cabin for his gun.

They were not having any luck with bear and had given up hope of catching one. On November 14, the trapper picked up the fresh tracks of a bear and gave it chase over very rough territory for a day, but never got close enough for a shot. By December 5 of 1920, Dick had enough of his learning experience. He learned the trapper was heading for Republic to get supplies. Dick was packed and ready to go when the trapper left.

Dick stayed in the hotel and talked to other people about the trapper. He learned the trapper was not highly thought of by the locals.

On December 6, Dick crossed paths with Rolland Ames in the Republic Post Office. Rolland was considered one of the greatest wolf and wilderness trappers in Michigan. Dick spent a week trapping and hunting with him.

On December 7, Dick and Rolland took a trip to Marquette to collect the bounty of $50 for a wolf. While collecting the bounty, Dick asked Deputy County Clerk Alice Beckman for the names of quality trappers in the area. She provided the names of Tom Sullivan, John Sterling, John Dingman, Ed Munson and Rolland Ames.

On December 8, Dick spent the night with Rolland at Jewell Beauchamp's house. On the next day, Dick and Rolland started walking to camp. It was an eighteen mile hike. Rolland's cabin was on the East Branch of the Fence River eighteen miles west of the old Witch Lake flag station on the railroad. It was on the west side of the river near the old sluice dam above the junction of the West and East branch. Rolland's foot was sore the following day, but they went down to Fence River, set traps and took pictures.

On December 10, Dick and Rolland went three and a half miles further down the Fence River and set mink and bobcat traps. The following day they went to West Branch and Bone Lake. Rolland found the tracks of a crippled gray wolf that had crossed the road in Green Timber. They also found that seven wolves had crossed Bone Lake on the ice. They planned to hunt them the next day but the weather did not cooperate for the next couple days. After the weather calmed, it took three days of tracking, but they finally got the crippled wolf.

Dick with a spike horn buck.

Dick wrote at least two articles about whether the wolf is dangerous - once in May of 1923 in Fur News and Outdoor World and once in May-June of 1926 in Wild Game Stories. Dick commented that any professional wolfer or trapper suggesting danger from wolf attacks was considered a joke. He made such a suggestion to Rolland and his response was "I wish they would try attacking me; I'd collect a lot more bounties than I do. It is hard enough to get sight of one."

During the winter of 1922-1923, Rolland Ames was found dead near his cabin by a state employed predatory animal hunter. His death either resulted from freezing or overexertion.

This photograph of Rolland Ames was used on the cover of the January 1924 issue of Fur News and Outdoor World.

Dick in northern Michigan after catching an ermine under a spruce tree. Note that he also had two mink furs dangling from the cartridge belt.

This photograph of Frank Peterson was used on the cover of a 1929 Triumph Trap brochure. A drawing of the photograph was also used on the cover of the December 1930 issue of Sportsman's Digest.

Dick met Frank Peterson at Rolland's place but did not have the opportunity to trap with him. Frank was an expert beaver trapper but the beaver season had closed. Dick commented Frank had two inch whiskers and a big Stetson hat with a beaded band. Dick thought he was very picturesque.

After a week of trapping with Rolland, Dick heard about other trappers in the area by the names of Charlie Shellman and Dick Sutliff. They were trapping by Dykes ranch. On the way to see them, Dick stopped and met Floyd Ames, Rolland's son. Dick spent a few days with Shellman and Sutliff.

Dick making a set in northern Michigan.

After his Michigan trap, Dick thought that the farmland trapper could make more money trapping muskrats and skunk than the expert trapper in the Upper Peninsula. Dick made the following observation - like the buffalo, the passenger pigeon and the beaver, the buckskin trapper would soon pass over the last long trail.

After returning from Michigan, Dick returned to the Cold River area in the Adirondacks. He gathered the traps, that had been cached over the summer, to trap the area again.

Dick worked for the Triumph Trap Company for four years. He was let go because of the disruption World War I had caused to business. A director's meeting was held and it was decided that the services of the field specialist, as well as that of several others, could be dispensed with. Dick was given a month's notice.

After his release, Dick was asked to apply for the advertising department of Oneida Community Ltd by Elmer Kreps who was Oneida's staff artist. Dick declined as he had already accepted the position of managing editor for Fur News in New York City. Dick and his family moved to New York City in 1921.

Dick referred to a quote from Elmer Kreps which summed up trapping in one sentence. "The trapper must know wild animals as a mother knows her child." Dick added that the trapper should know wild animals so well they can not only read their trail signs, but guess their future movements.

Dick setting a big pan Kangaroo Triumph trap.

Chapter 3. Fur News

Dick in New York City.

One of the Dick's first articles with photographs was published in the March 1917 issue of the Fur News. The article was titled "Notes from Holston" referring to his family's property in Virginia. Amongst the many topics he covered, Dick discussed the lateness of the magazine and that it was "getting on

This photograph, taken at the Duck Hole cabin, was used on the header for Dick's "Trail Tested and Right" articles. The photograph was reversed in the magazine.

our nerves" as the previous December issue had not arrived. This comment was an omen about changes to the magazine which would occur in 1921.

Dick made his first visit to talk to the Fur News staff in June of 1917 while working for the Triumph Trap Company. From 1917 to 1921, Dick wrote numerous articles for Fur News along with contributing many photographs. Many were used on the front cover and throughout the magazine including in advertising for different companies. He had some series articles. A Trapper's Musings ran for a little over a year starting in November of 1918. The topics covered varied considerably from women to nicotine and from trapping to diggings skunks out of their holes.

"Tripping the Wicomico" was a five-part series about Dick's trip to trap the Wicomico River in Maryland. In his book "The Narratives of Trapping Life", Dick includes this article but the title includes the word "Trapping" instead of "Tripping". There could have been a spelling error in the first article in the magazine and Dick decided to leave it as Tripping in the rest of the series but corrected it when the book was published.

Dick's outreach efforts increased advertising income.

"Trapper's Equipment" and "Trail Tested and Right" were both series articles about different equipment for the trapper and outdoorsman. The equipment covered was quite variable and ranged from lights and camping equipment to binoculars and life saving kits.

In August of 1920, Dick added "and Outdoor World" to the name of the magazine. The magazine included more fishing and hunting articles along with

This advertisement of Dick pulling a toboggan was used several times in 1924 issues of Fur News and Outdoor World, but the message in the white rectangle was different in each issue.

the usual trapping articles.

In April or May of 1921, Dick became the managing editor. He added color to covers or more accurately, Beulah did. She used water colors to color in parts of the cover photos.

Dick increased advertising revenue and decreased the size of the magazine. The smaller size reduced the delivery time so the readership would have less opportunity for lateness to "get on their nerves".

In the July 1921 issue of the Writer's Monthly, Dick is noted as being the new managing editor. It also notes the magazine had been slow in reporting in the past, but under Dick's management, it would be more prompt.

Original photograph is on the left. Cover with a fox added by Dick is on the right.

From 1921 to 1924, Dick's articles increased in diversity including more articles on hunting, fishing, camping, hiking, wildlife information and photography along with the usual trapping articles. His other series articles ended and a new series article called "A Trapper's Country" started. This article was about Dick's trip to Michigan to stay with the trapper that had made himself out to be more of a trapper than he really was.

In the September 1922 issue, the editor discusses Dick's yearning to be back in the field and out of the office in New York City. The editor states "Dick is a rambler, always looking for the Trapper's Mecca".

In the fall of 1923, Dick made a trapping trip to the Bad Lands of the western states. He found his most profitable trapping was done in the coulees or gullies. Coulees confined the animal's activities, provided many narrow spots on trails for trap sets, and provided a sandy bottom facilitating trap setting.

Dick commented that setting the ordinary trails on the plains was impossible as the cattle often sprung the traps. A few cattle trails crossed the coulees, but as long as Dick set his traps away from the crossings, he did not have sprung traps.

Dick used a pony called Fleetfoot for transportation. The pony carried all of Dick's supplies and traps. Dick would locate places to set traps from Fleetfoot's back and only leave the pony's back to make sets.

Dick was mainly after coyotes, but also caught bobcats, badgers, fox, skunks and opossums. Dick also caught a few raccoons.

This black and white photograph of Dick fishing the Cowasselon River in New York had color added by Beulah using water colors. It was on the cover of the May 1921 issue.

This cartoon titled "How contributors are spending their summer" was used in the July 1917 issue.

This Peter Unprime cartoon was used in October 1918 issue.

Dick was the managing editor until November 1924. The publisher offered to sell the magazine to Dick and the staff editor, but as noted in the 1922 editorial, Dick had enough of city life. The magazine was finally sold to A. R. Harding with ownership changing with the August 1925 issue.

In November of 1924, Dick packed his belongings from his six room Morningside Avenue apartment and shipped them back to his mother's place outside Hiltons, Virginia. He loaded his wife and six-year-old child into the Hupp roadster, and headed into the winter weather of the Adirondacks. Part of his belongings shipped to Hiltons included a 3,000 volume book collection. Dick had become a collector of rare books about Western Americana while in New York.

Dick believed that books about Western Americana were becoming scarcer and more valuable each year. Dick discussed that small pamphlets, the books printed for distribution on trains or books that cost less than a dollar in the second-hand book stalls, then considered junk, were just a few years later considered valuable records of a time that has past and gone into history. These books were often rare and bringing fabulous prices. Dick thought that those who had a collection of books on Western Americana, not only had an interesting library, but also had a profitable investment.

Part of Dick's book collection.

Dick had studied cold weather camping and did not see any reason why motor camping could not be adapted to winter weather. This was his opportunity to show Beulah snow covered peaks. She had never seen the beauty of the northern winter woods

Dick behind the wheel in New York City.

The family crossed the Hudson River on the Fort Lee ferry. Luckily, they only had a short wait before it arrived. They had gotten a late start and the weather was unfavorable when they began. Instead of making a camp in the dark, the three stopped at the home of some good friends in Florham Park, New Jersey.

They did not get an early start the next morning either. That morning Dick and Beulah argued about whether to go north or south. If the weather was pleasant, they would have started toward Virginia.

Dick headed north out of Florham Park. As he turned onto the state highway, Beulah called his attention to the flock of geese flying southward. Beulah said that the geese were heading the way that the Wood family should be going. Dick responded that they would be going that way soon enough as he stepped on the gas.

They lunched in Suffern, New York where the restaurant was selected mostly because of parking convenience. The car was parked in sight of their table. Dick had over $500 worth of cameras, binoculars, and other loose articles lying about in the car. After lunch, they traveled through Tuxedo Park to Newburgh and camped three miles beyond after buying a few groceries in town. The family camped in a public campground with a lake. Signs were posted saying that there was no bathing in the lake but fishing was allowed. A boat was anchored to the bank that could be used by tourists for free.

After continuing, the three found that some additional clothing was needed for the cold. They stopped in Albany and purchased a sheepskin lined top coat and lined gauntlet driving gloves for Dick along with an oversized pair of shoes for Inez so she could wear more than one pair of socks.

The family reached the municipal campground in Schenectady after dark. A traffic officer directed them to the campground that was on the east end of Central Park. An attendant showed them where to camp, find running water and showed them the new $25,000 casino. Dick said that the family felt perfectly at home and that it felt like they were camping on the upper end of Central Park, Manhattan not Schenectady.

Early the next morning, Dick took the road northward through Saratoga Springs and Glen Falls. After passing Glen Falls, the surroundings began to take on the aspect of the northland with evergreen forests. They passed through Lake George. After passing through Warrensburg, the family pulled into a state campground because it was nearly dark. The campground had stone fireplaces and refuse cans conveniently located.

The next morning, they proceeded through Chestertown and east toward Lake Champlain by way of Brant Lake. The road took them over a high mountain. It was a macadam road and in excellent condition. The highway followed this lake for four miles and then the road began to ascend rapidly. Half way up the mountain, Dick stopped for water at a state marked spring. A sign was posted instructing visitors to fill their radiators there. A long steep grade was ahead which they ascended nicely in high gear. The cool weather kept the motor from overheating.

Beulah tuning in the radio for the daily news, in lieu of a newspaper, while camping. This photograph was used in the article titled "Northern Trek" in the July 1925 issue of Motor Camper & Tourist.

The family passed through Crown Point and traveled on to Elizabethtown by way of Westport and back down the valley road. They took the road to Blue Ridge. The road, through rugged mountains, was gravel but graded well with good drainage.

The goal of following this road was to visit the Boreas River country which was were Dick did his first trapping in the Adirondacks and learned of the Cold River area. They camped at a state campground in sight of the Boreas River. Dick commented that before the road was opened to tourists, the river had remarkable trout fishing. He suspected that it was still better than the average trout stream.

Wolf Pond, where Dick set his first traps in the Adirondacks, was a thirty minute walk to the north. He talked to a guide who managed a stopping point for hunters at the Boreas River. The guide trapped beaver, otter, fisher and other furbearers within walking distance of his house. They discussed a beaver dam on the Wolf Pond outlet. The family stayed here several days hiking and boating.

The family continued through Tahawus and north to Henderson Lake. The road ended at the Tahawus Club property. There was not a public campground, but camping was permitted on any state-owned land. The state had marked several trails leading to Cold River. Dick and a sportsman from Elizabethtown hiked as far as Preston Ponds and camped out under the stars on the west shore of that body of water. Beulah and Inez stayed with the automobile and main camp at the end of the road.

The next day, the family retraced their route and traveled toward Newcomb where they stopped for gas. The three continued to Rich Lake and camped at a shack on Fishing Brook. Dick had just gotten the tent set up when it started to rain.

The weather was getting wintery and Dick was afraid he would get stuck on one of the unimproved roads, so he backtracked to Elizabethtown. From there they proceeded north through Keeseville and Plattsburg, then from West Chazy to Malone. He called this area typical North Country with dairy farms and stones everywhere.

They continued down the west side of the Adirondacks and camped overnight near Canton. They continued on the highway by Gouverneur, Carthage and Lowville. By the time they reached Boonville, a steady snow was falling.

Dick called a friend in Utica to see about stopping. The friend said they had a dinner dance at the Hotel Utica and invited Dick and the family to attend. After that, the family resided in an apartment in Chattanooga, Tennessee for the winter.

Dr Claude P. "Doc" Fordyce.

Dick combined two of his favorite activities, camping and driving a car, into an activity which took up much of his time and provided information for several articles. Dick credits Dr. Claude P. "Doc" Fordyce with introducing him to Bear Mountain Park and convincing him that camping, rather than a means to an end, was a major sport in itself.

This tent was designed by Dr. Claude P. Fordyce and made by Dick Whall.

Dick credits Elmer Kreps with blazing the trail. Dick utilized the book Camp and Trail Methods written by Elmer. Dick embraced a quote from Horace Kephart, who Dick called the father of camping lore. The quote was "The more one carries in his head, the less he needs to carry in his packsack."

Some of Dick's sportsmen friends had dubbed him "The Camper". A nomadic life afield had a peculiar lure to him. He was always looking for a wilderness mecca. He had camped from Ontario to the mango groves of Florida. His interest was facilitated by reading Nessmuk's Woodcraft, Thoreau's Walden, Dudley Warner's Life in the Wilderness and Paine's Tent Dweller.

The trailer folded out into the camper seen later in this book.

Camping in the Adirondacks. Dick is on the right and E.J. is on the left in this photograph. The third person is a trapping student.

Bear Mountain from Palisades Interstate Park in 1924.

Camping at Palisades Interstate Park in 1924

Dick fell in love with motor camping while living in New York City. He did not like jobs that revolved around a desk. He felt compelled to get outdoors at every opportunity and accordingly, invested in a motor car. He explored the surrounding country. One weekend in 1924, Dick, Beulah, and Inez found Palisades Interstate Park located forty miles north of the city on the west side of the Hudson. The Palisades Park experience was the forerunner of trips around the country and numerous articles. Once Dick got a taste of the fascinating and independent life of the motor camper, he threw off the shackles of despondency resulting from the confinement and routine of an office job.

Dick was initiated to driving an automobile on the busy roads between Albany and Syracuse, and Binghamton and Ogdensburg. He said he took a postgraduate course in New York City and specifically cites trying to beat a New York Taxi driver to a corner as the final test that he failed. That accident cost him $500 that went to the men who hammer out dents and replace broken parts.

Dick became disgusted with New York City travel as every road was always busy. His attitude toward his automobile changed when he adapted it to camping, hunting and fishing. It was home to him and his family on many motor camping trips.

Automobile in accident in Oneida on August 6, 1919.

In the September 1924 issue of Motor Camper & Tourist, Dick's article titled "Go LIGHT Motor Camping" describes how he got into an accident requiring the purchase of his new Hupp Roadster. The accident occurred on August 6, 1919 in Oneida. Dick was driving his car north on Main Street when the car skidded due to slippery pavement from a sudden rain. The car rammed a wooden trolley wire pole north of St. Patrick's Church. Neither Dick nor his male occupant were hurt.

The auto struck the pole with such force that the pole broke off at the ground. The left fender of the car was smashed, the frame buckled, the transmission cracked and had considerable other damage. The vehicle was taken to Coles Tool and Machine Company for repairs.

Dick in his Hupp Roadster.

In 1926, Dick went into the Smoky Mountains as far as the rough mountain road extended up Mt Mitchell, the highest point east of the Mississippi River. He followed an abandoned lumber company railroad bed. Dick proceeded even further away from civilization by following the stream bed for several miles. Finally, he was stopped by an unfinished trestle spanning a gorge.

As of July 1926, Dick had visited thirty states and the Hupp roadster had taken him to each. The vehicle originally cost $1,800. Dick said he made a wager with the Missus that he could continue to run one of "them things".

Dick drove his Hupp Roadster off road as well as on paved roads. He drove it into the Adirondacks, Blue Ridges, Cumberland Mountains, Ozarks and the Smoky Mountains right to the banks of trout streams. He wanted to get to areas that were remote, away from highways and railroads, so that the size and number of pursued game increased.

Dick plowed through gumbo clay to the axles in Nebraska and Kansas. He drove over huge imbedded rocks where the running gears dragged. After all his experiences driving the Hupp Roadster, he looked at his automobile differently. Dick said he and the roadster became as intimate as two peas in a pod and there were no secrets between them. Dick thoroughly tested the capabilities of each vehicle he owned.

Dick and Beulah camping in a remote area of the Smoky Mountains.

Chapter 5. Superior National Forest

Dick's trip into Superior National Forest included canoeing, camping and cooking. This photograph shows those aspects of the trip. Note the canoe in the middle right of the photograph.

In June 1925, Dick had just returned from fishing with Ernest H. Peckinpaugh at Little River and convinced Beulah to take a five month motor camping trip as far north as Superior National Forest in Minnesota, as far west as Falls City, Nebraska and return through the Ozarks. They had been living in an apartment in Chattanooga and were looking for a way to beat the summer heat. Dick pointed out that they would save on rent, entertainment, cooking and he could make some money by writing as they went along.

On the way, the family did some fishing in the Cumberland River at Pineville, Kentucky. They traveled on the Dixie Highway through the bluegrass section of Kentucky. Dick drove through Ohio, Indiana and Illinois on good roads. The three followed the National Old Trail and the Lincoln Highway. The facilities for tourists were abundant. Dick had fond memories of the barbeque sandwiches sold by Ohio roadside stands.

There were good roads through Chicago and into Wisconsin. Camp sites were plentiful and campers welcome. Just west of Hudson, Wisconsin on the St. Croix River, they crossed into Minnesota. After being in Minnesota a short time, a sign met their eyes stating "Welcome: Non-residents are required to register. No charge. Register here. Fishing licenses available."

Dick stopped to register and bought a fishing license which cost $3. He figured later that he had beaten the state out of $25 worth of fish. A Game and Fish employee said the money from non-resident fishermen was spent entirely for fish propagation and restocking purposes.

Dick also got a sixty day permit to tour and live in the state of Minnesota without being bothered by motor cops or tax collectors. They left and soon were in St. Paul. Dick was scheduled to make some calls in Minneapolis. He was running low on gas money and remembered that a Minneapolis editor owed him.

The family was going to spend the night at Minnehaha Park. They made slow time in traffic and hit road construction. When it was dark, Beulah recommended that Dick stop and get directions. He wanted an excuse to buy a smoke anyway. The drug store vendor gave them directions and they were off again. They passed Fort Snelling and then heading north, they found the park and set up camp.

The family was met by hordes of mosquitoes. After getting the camp set up, Dick quickly got two buckets of water. He fastened up the tent for the night. The family doped up with Unguentine and ate supper.

The following day, Dick explored Minneapolis and got some gas money from the editor. He headed the roadster north by way of Robbinsdale, and collected more money owed to him by a publisher. Because of the money he collected, they extended their time in Minnesota to four weeks instead of the planned two.

On July 3 1925, the family left Minneapolis via Highway 5 toward Isanti. They camped at Harris after making 85 miles for the day. The campground was on a wooden knoll just off the highway. Fresh eggs and milk were procured at a nearby farm house. Dick found dairy products inexpensive in Minnesota.

On July 4, there was heavy traffic as they continued north. Dick commented that right angle turns were common on the roads in Minnesota. They came upon an overturned automobile at a turn with its wheels still spinning. Dick slowed down to get through but held his speed at 30 miles per hour.

Dick went around traffic at Duluth by taking a short cut road leading north off Highway 5. They took Road No. 11 out of Duluth and followed it to Virginia. They continued to Cook and then left the main highway following 24 to Elbow Lake. Dick stopped at a locked two car plank garage and noted a path leading down to a boat landing where two row boats were tied.

The family loaded their equipment into a boat and rowed for the opposite shore. They arrived at Lingerlonger Camp in time for one of Mrs. Burris' famous suppers.

Lingerlonger Camp cabin.

Beulah and Inez are on the right side of the group of people.

Beulah and Inez stayed at Lingerlonger Camps while Dick and Jack Burris took a two hundred mile canoe trip through Superior National Forest following the Little Indian Sioux route. Jack was a game warden and state trapper of predatory animals in the Superior National Forest. In addition, he had a summer business renting cabins and boats to visitors of Elbow Lake. Jack had the only resort on the lake.

Jack on the Black River after leaving Black Lake.

On July 10 at 8:15 am, Dick and Jack left from Lingerlonger Camps. They portaged the bulk of their items to Black Lake the day before. They proceeded across Black Lake and into Black Bay on Vermillion Lake. Dick and Jack lunched at an old Indian camp on that bay. They continued and camped for the night on the sheltered side of an island in Norwegian Bay. Dick noted that the northern pike were feeding on swarms of flies.

Dick and Jack left camp the next day at 7:30 am. They paddled down Vermillion Lake past several resorts. The two stopped for lunch on an island in Niles Bay after passing the Grandview Resort. From there they headed due south and passed through Muskrat Channel. Dick and Jack followed the north shore and reached Trout Lake. George Lott hauled their outfit over the portage with a horse and cart for $1.50. Once in Trout Lake, they paddled up the lake against the wind and camped on a point of the mainland.

On July 12, Dick and Jack paddled up Trout Lake searching for the channel to Little Trout Lake. They fished along the way but did not have any luck. The two paddled into East Bay and Jack insisted the channel must be in the bay. He spotted a deer swimming across the bay. They tried, unsuccessfully, to paddle within distance to take a photograph. The chase ended near the proper channel. They finally caught a couple of walleye while in the bay.

Jack on Black Bay of Vermillion Lake. This photograph was used in the Outdoor Recreation magazine. In the magazine, the Lingerlonger Camps wording was removed from the canoe.

Camping on Lake Vermillion.

The Little Indian Sioux Portage.

Dick and Jack portaged to Little Indian Sioux River. The portage was one and a quarter miles, the toughest of the trip so far. They took lunch while completing the portage. The portage started at 10:30 am and finished at 4:30 pm.

Dick noted that it was a grueling portage in the hot sun. At least half of the portage was over poles laid in the bog.

Little Indian Sioux River.

Dick and Jack finally launched in Little Indian Sioux River. It had started to rain and they paddled through the drizzle.

It was only a short run and they had to portage again into Bootleg Lake. They camped at that portage on rough ground. The mosquitoes were fierce from the last portage to this camp.

The next morning, they were up early anticipating the reputed excellent bass fishing in Bootleg Lake. Ironically, Bootleg Lake had a creek which dumped into it named Triumph. Dick and Jack completed the portage of a little over a mile in the hottest weather of the trip. They passed a cabin on the shore and ate lunch there. Jack napped at the cabin while Dick fished. He caught several bass up to two pounds and a four pound northern pike.

They camped at the cabin. At midnight, it stormed fiercely and everything in the tent got wet.

On July 14, they started downstream with the wet duffle spread out to dry on the canoe. After passing the Little Indian Sioux River Falls, they caught a bull moose in the water. The moose saw the canoe and swam downstream for one hundred yards then took to land. Dick got a few photos, but sadly, these would not turn out. They ate lunch on the river. That afternoon, the two paddled back to the falls looking to spot the moose for more pictures, but did not find it.

Photograph was used in an article titled "Camping is a Sport" in the January 1935 issue of Sports Afield.

Dick and Jack did not leave camp the next day until 9:00 am because they were getting caught up on lost sleep. They had two portages right away and paddled against a heavy head wind. The river broadened and they made several portages around rapids. Late in the day, they came to docks at a portage and well made trails. Dick and Jack camped for the night in a clump of virgin timber.

Dick and Jack started out at noon on July 16. They surprised a young bull moose feeding near Pauness Lake. Five minutes later, they saw another one. They made camp on the lakeshore and had a quick lunch. They did some trolling catching a northern pike and a walleye. Jack cooked a big meal while Dick took pictures around the camp.

Dick and Jack started out at 6:00 pm and Dick spotted a deer on a point across the lake. As they approached the deer, they saw two deer on hind feet fighting or playing. The two trolled back to the camp and caught a northern pike on the way. Dick commented that deer were snorting near the tent while he wrote by candle light.

On July 17, they went back and saw the moose in the same place as the day before. The wind was against them. The moose started walking toward the woods while Dick and Jack were still three hundred yards away. Dick snapped a picture of it. They paddled through a channel in a point of land and down the bay to a portage that lead into another part of the lake. Dick called this a wild area off the canoe route. They paddled to the regular portage and got started at 11:00 am. They portaged northwest for a quarter of a mile into Loon Lake. They lunched on an island in Loon Lake and picked some blueberries for desert.

Dick and Jack headed west for the outlet to Loon River. They could not find it and explored several bays looking for the outlet. Dick caught a five pound northern pike.

On July 18, the two started back to the west bay and got a picture of a brown bear on a rock ledge. It was the right bay and they continued to the portage to Loon River. It was less than a quarter mile long. They passed a Canadian Ranger Station. There Dick bought bacon, lard and coffee from a woman. The river was high and they floated over three portages shown on their map. They camped for the night on a point in Little Vermillion Narrows. Dick saw two porcupines fighting while camping.

On Sunday, July 19, Dick and Jack were up at 6:00 am and in the canoe at 8:00 am. They paddled down Sandpoint Lake and King William Narrows into Crane Lake. They portaged into Vermillion River at noon. The one and a half mile portage was done by 2:00 pm. Dick and Jack paddled through one rapids and portaged two more. They camped for the night at another portage.

Dick and Jack slept late on July 20. Once started, they paddled upstream into a head wind all day. They landed at the last portage before reaching the Pelican River. That portage included a steep climb with hordes of mosquitoes.

Dick stood in Canada to take this photograph while Jack peeled potatoes in the United States.

Dick frying walleye on Canadian soil at Little Vermillion Narrows.

136

They hastily built two fires and set up the tent at a campsite.

On 21 July, Dick and Jack passed a lumber camp early in the day and reached Pelican River in the rain. They stopped at the falls near the mouth of the Pelican into the Vermillion and fished catching several northern pike and a walleye. Dick caught eleven northern pike out of twelve casts with the smallest being six pounds. They cleaned the fish while being harassed by mosquitoes.

Dick commented that the Vermillion River portages were very rocky, steep and rough. The Pelican River portages were covered with vegetation and showed little travel. Dick found the Pelican River more interesting than the Vermillion River but it was hard paddling against a current most of the way.

Dick and Jack made camp near an old lumber camp and heard wolves yelping at bedtime. A cold front came through that evening and they nearly froze. They got up at 5:00 am and thawed out by the fire. Breakfast included the last of the coffee and bacon.

In the afternoon, Dick and Jack reached several rapids. They ran over some and waded through others. Dick missed the best opportunity to take photographs of a deer because his camera was in its case. They reached Rice Lake at 4:30 pm and ate at 5:00 pm. They stalled in the rice beds searching for the outlet. At 7:30, the two camped on a virgin spot in swampy land.

On Thursday, July 23, Dick and Jack paddled through reeds, rice and lily pads until noon. They finally reached the Elbow Lake portage. The portage was a third of a mile long. Dick missed another camera opportunity with a deer in Elbow River because Jack was coughing.

Dick commented that this was a pretty river of lily pads and marshy evergreen shores. They passed bear cubs near Gheen's farm. The western end of Elbow Lake was full of lily pads. They had a two and a half mile paddle through narrows and down the lake to Lingerlonger Camps. Dick and Jack completed the two hundred mile trip in thirteen days.

Unknown to Dick, his camera malfunctioned during this trip and none of the photographs turned out. He did not test the camera shutter because it had been working properly before the trip. Weeks later when he developed the film, Dick found that all his photographs, including many close-up shots, were blurry. He determined that the camera shutter had simply slowed down 50% with age.

On 25 July, the family left Lingerlonger Camps and arrived at Cook at about dark. They camped four miles south of town. The next day was Sunday and they slept late. At 10:25, they finished a breakfast of June berries and hit the road. Five miles south of where they camped, Dick turned off No. 11 onto 22 as a shortcut to Chisholm. This road had bad wash board bumps necessitating the installation of a new spring. Dick carried enough parts to overhaul his automobile and had an extra front spring in the rear luggage compartment.

Jack was busy at Lingerlonger Camps the entire year. A man and dog pull a boat attached to a sled over the frozen lake surface.

At Chisholm, they were on No. 8 which was a macadam road for eight miles, then concrete to Hibbing. They camped at Grand Rapids having made 81 miles for the day.

The following day they passed Deer River and saw the sign for Cut Foot Sioux Lake. It was fourteen miles north on No. 12. Dick thought with a name so unique, it deserved investigation. They pulled into a Forest Reserve campground at William's Narrows. Dick trolled for half a day without any bites.

Dick fishing at Itasca State Park.

The family left Cut Foot Sioux Lake at 11:00 am on July 28. They continued south on No. 8 past Cass Lake and into Bemidji where they left for Itasca State Park on No. 4. The three arrived just in time to get the camp set up before it started to rain. Another camper asked to borrow Dick's axe to drive in his tent stakes. Dick noted that the axe was returned.

On July 29, Dick fished with a couple of acquaintances and they caught a couple of northern pike. While Dick was fishing, Beulah and Inez were entertained by the rangers' menagerie. The family spent a very enjoyable day at this campground. Dick photographed elk, fly fish in the headwaters of the Mississippi River, and visit the Forest Rangers' club house.

The next day, the family made camp at Weirs on Little Mantrap Lake. Dick had to pass up fishing on this lake because of lack of time. They arrived in Park Rapids after leaving Weirs.

On August 1 of 1925, they camped at Osakis Lake. As the family left the next morning, they came to a bridge that crossed the outlet of the lake. There were several fishermen there catching sunfish. Dick had to stop and fish. Before he knew it, it was noon. Dick and Beulah caught about a dozen sunfish and motored to a shady grove. The fish were cleaned and cooked. Dick said that the dinner of fresh fish on the bank of Osakis Lake was one of the highlights of the trip.

That evening, August 2, the family camped in Sunburg Municipal Campground. They headed out the next morning and passed Willmar. On August 3, they left Minnesota and headed for Spirit and Okoboji lakes in Iowa.

In the fall of 1925, the family traveled from Fall City, Nebraska to Red Bank, Tennessee. The trip took one month and covered 1191 miles. The roads varied from mud to paved and resulted in numerous tire repairs. The trip included numerous river crossings on ferries.

Before they left Fall City, they attended a rodeo. On Thursday, September 17, they did not leave until 2:45 pm as Dick was preparing letters and photos for the mail. The family camped in Effingham, Kansas that night. On Friday, they arrived in Kansas City on a very hot day. The temperature was 100 degrees. They ate in town and camped after dark.

On Saturday, Dick made calls around town and stopped at the Auto Club on Main Street. He got 2 quarts of oil for free and paid $0.17 a gallon for gas. Dick paid $.25 to camp on dusty bare ground that night.

On Sunday, September 20, they headed south out of Kansas City and went through Louisburg. The family lunched by the road near Fort Scott, Kansas and made a stop at Joplin, Missouri. They camped in the yard of a school house on a hill near Neosho. The road was a wide, well graded, gravel road that paralleled a river.

On Monday, they passed through Lanagan, Missouri where there were cabins for rent from $15 to $37.50 per week at Mystery Cave. The cave had an entrance fee of $0.75. They stopped at Indian River to swim and take photographs. Then they crossed the Indian River on a pontoon bridge.

The family arrived in Bentonville, Arkansas, and camped in a free campground two blocks north of the highway. The mosquitoes were bad in the wooded park. The campgrounds were fairly clean and had water and lights. They camped next to a "greenhorn" from Oklahoma who could not set up his new $9.50 shed type tent by himself.

As they left Bentonville on Tuesday, Dick stopped to get a quart of oil and was charged a $1.00 too much. He went back and collected once he determined this.

They drove through apple orchards on a high plateau all day. The family entered rough mountains soon after leaving Rogers. They ate lunch in the woods by the roadside. Dick took a wrong turn in Eureka Springs.

Dick met a Mr. Yocum from Reedy, Arkansas on a hill outside of Eureka Springs. He was migrating to Oklahoma in a covered wagon. Mr. Yocum had his motherless children and household effects in the wagon including a wash tub fastened underneath the wagon and an iron kettle fastened on the back.

On September 22, they camped for free in a park with well water at Green Forest. The family had not been there for two hours when representatives of the village community stopped to inquire if the family needed anything. Dick accepted an invitation to walk home with a farmer and help himself to some apples. Dick filled a sack and reached into his coin pocket. The farmer said that the apples did not cost anything and when they were gone, Dick could come back and help himself.

Beulah at the Indian River with Inez in the background.

The family stayed there for three days while it rained. They stayed over Saturday and Sunday waiting for the roads to dry up. Dick worked on an article about touring and another about camera use for Outing magazine.

Dick finished up the articles and got them ready to mail, so they did not start out until about noon on Monday, September 28. The road was under construction from Harrison to ten miles outside of Bellefonte.

This ferry was located by Madisonville, Tennessee. This photograph was taken a few years after this trip. Ferries could not compete with new bridges and quickly went by the wayside.

The family camped for free at Yellville right in the center of town. They bought supplies and started out at 9:00 am on Tuesday. The car had a flat tire at Flippin. The road in this area had signs noting the name of the road as B.V.D. Inez commented that that company sure did advertise.

They took ferries across the White and North Fork rivers. They were both swollen due to recent rains. The ferrymen on the North Fork ferry were noticeably anxious about the safety of their boat. Dick's car stalled on the east bank of the river and may have slid back into the river had the anchored ferry not held the car until the men sanded the road. Dick thought this was a dangerous crossing and should either be condemned or put in safe condition when the new highway was finished.

Road between Yellville and Mountain Home.

Dick thought they were trail blazers having left the highway at Yellville and taken a proposed road, driving past construction gangs. Dick drove over a mountain wagon road. Locals did not know whether an automobile could get through to Mountain Home. The family made it by abusing a good car. Dick commented that he felt the running boards dragging over rocks in many places.

Dick and family camped at Viola on October 4, 1925. In Viola, they visited with Cora Burns and family. The road improved after Viola but not by much as it was not more than a rough wagon road. At least, small cars had been going over it.

Dick had not seen a car track on the forty miles of road west of Viola. The rain storm, they had weathered in Green Forest, had obliterated all car tracks and almost the entire road. The gullies were so deep in places that Dick had to straddle them to prevent the axles from dragging on the ground. If the road had not had a large quantity of stones, it would have been washed away.

Hogs disputed the right of way with Dick on the road in northern Arkansas.

The family went through Salem on October 5. Just west of Doniphan they encountered the Current River. They camped there for the night and did some fishing. Dick called it "the famous fly-rod stream". They crossed the Current River on October 6. The family camped at Dexter, Missouri in a free public campground that evening.

On October 7, Dick took the road to New Madrid. It was gravel and full of chuck holes. It rained all day and a local said it had rained for a month. They were turned back from Lilburn due to high water and had to find a different route into New Madrid. Dick described New Madrid as a dead looking town.

The family camped on the Mississippi River, in an open field, under a pecan tree at New Madrid. In New Madrid, no one knew definitely about the roads to Tiptonville, Tennessee. They left camp at 8:30 am on the morning of October 8 to wait for the ferry to cross over the Mississippi River into Tennessee.

145

Although this ferry was located at Blythe which is eight miles above Birchwood, Tennessee on the Tennessee River, it still gives the reader a glimpse of the challenges with crossing large rivers long ago.

Dick asked Dick Carrington, the ferryman, about the roads to Tiptonville, Tennessee. Carrington said they were passable. Dick noted that they were ferried over for $2 and "set adrift in a jungle". The car had to be pushed up the muddy bank on the Tennessee side by a group of men. The car almost got stuck in a mud hole in sight of the ferry. The car then had a blowout. Dick changed the tire and proceeded through mud holes along the levee.

After a few miles, the road veered off through cotton fields. The car was seldom out of second gear and could barely get through some of the mud holes. Dick had to cross back over the levee once to dodge a large hole. After two or three miles, they hit regular gumbo and had about fourteen miles of the worst roads possible.

The car had three blowouts within five miles of Tiptonville and they had to run on the flats to get to town at dark. Including these three, Dick paid for six tire repairs so far on the trip. The license plate for the car was lost traveling the sixteen miles west of Tiptonville. Dick called this the worst part of the trip. They camped in a vacant lot by a house.

On October 9, they were at Tiptonville, Tennessee. On October 10, the family was at Blue Bank on Reelfoot Lake. On October 11, they were at Samburg on Reelfoot Lake. The family did some fishing and Dick caught a 5 ½ pound bass.

146

Beulah holding the bass that Dick caught at Reelfoot Lake.

On October 12, the family ate lunch at Union City and camped between Dresden and McKinnie. The camp was on a hillside nine miles west of McKinnie. The family took a ferry across the Tennessee River and they camped near McEwen. On the October 13, they camped near Murphysboro. On October 14 and 15, they traveled between Murphysboro and Chattanooga.

This ferry was at Loudon, Tennessee. The photograph was taken a few years after this trip.

County road near McMinnville, Tennessee.

On October 16, the family arrived in the North Chattanooga area and lived at 3807 Oweda Terrace in Red Bank. They built a house there. The garage was built first.

House in Red Bank.

The family lived in the garage and stored their furniture in tents until the house was done. They lived here until Dick retired in 1960 except for a short time in Parkside, Pennsylvania.

Rock landscaping.

Besides his many other outdoor interests, Dick collected rocks. He incorporated them in landscaping around their house in Red Bank. One house project, of which he was particularly proud, was a side patio he created using stone and concrete. Dick purchased the flat rocks for the top surface.

Side patio

This photograph was used in an advertisement for Graflex Cameras in the May 1930 issue of Popular Science Monthly and in the article titled "Raccoons for the Amateur Fur Farmer" in the January 1923 issue of Fur News and Outdoor World.

Chapter 6. Elric J. Dailey

Dick with E.J. This photograph was used as the cover on February 1933 issue of Fur Fish Game.

Dick and E.J. met while working for the Triumph Trap Company. They trapped together for several years and kept in touch for many years after that. Their partnership is best known for the time they trapped together in the Cold River country. E.J. recalled his time in the Cold River area as the hardest of times and the best of times. He had youthful legs and hundred dollar fisher, blizzards and dead calm forty below mornings when the snow squeaked underfoot and his breath rose straight up.

In the article titled "Trapping Wages on Home Grounds" in the March 1920 issue of Fur News, Dick tells a story about E.J. going on the "warpath" as another trapper had stolen a mink and set in the swamp E.J. was trapping. He found a mink escaped from a trap. He found tracks, other than his, in the snow and some traps set in the area. He quickly deduced this other trapper removed the mink from his trap.

E.J. returning from checking his traps.

E.J. went to the head of the stream feeding the swamp and set several traps to catch any mink travelling into the marsh from that direction. He did the same thing where the stream flowed out of the swamp. In the middle of the swamp, there was high ground where an old stone fence approached the stream at a right angle. E.J. noticed several traps set on land for weasel. They were set in plain view along the fence and around the edges of a cedar thicket.

EJ checking a stone fence for weasel sign.

E.J. crawled on hands and knees under dense brush until he reached the stone wall and made some sets. This location cut off any weasels traveling toward the other person's traps. He pulled his traps that were close to the other traps.

E.J. checked his traps and found he had caught two mink and a weasel. The other trapper had vacated the area. Dick believed he had left because he could not catch anything. He also believed that if E.J would not have pulled the traps that were close to the other person's traps, E.J.'s traps would have been gone as well.

E.J. with part of his 1937 catch at Jo Indian Pond. Note the pet red fox on the left side of photograph. The photograph was used in the article titled "A Mixed Trapline" in the September 1938 issue of Fur Fish Game.

A sign of their continuing partnership beyond the Adirondacks is in the January 1930 issue of the Hunter-Trader-Trapper. On the page showing the contents of that issue, a story with the title of "The Trapper Afloat" showing E.J. Dailey as the writer was included. On the first page of the article, Dick Wood was noted as the writer. The editor was confused as to who should be credited for writing the article.

154

E.J. with fox.

In the fall of 1930, Dick ran a trap line with E.J. around Jo Indian Pond in the Adirondacks near the Racquette River within 10 miles of both the upper St. Regis and the Grass rivers. They used an automobile and covered about 100

miles in a day. The two men set traps for mink, muskrat, coon and fox. The line was checked for a few weeks. Dick was scheduled to leave by the beginning of December. It was lucky he left when planned as a foot of snow fell during his trip out.

E.J. used an experience with Dick to explain a trapper's instinct to locate traps in rugged territory. E.J. and Dick put out traps in a 1000 acre marsh covered with reeds. Dick said sign was scarce and that he made only one set. E.J. asked Dick how he would find the trap. Dick said it would be easy because he had bent a reed over.

E.J.'s Oswegatchie River cabin.

E.J.'s main trapping cabin was located near Jo Indian Pond. The cabin was located near the outlet of this pond into the Racquette River. The cabin was hidden amongst giant pines with a rough and hilly dirt road leading to it. The building had tar paper walls with three rooms heated by two stoves. One room was a sleeping porch where E.J. dried the skins during season.

In the article titled "The Winter Trapline" in the December 1930 issue of Sportsman's Digest, E.J. uncharacteristically uses Dick's name in the article. E.J. routinely used alias for the trappers that accompanied him. Locations were also changed.

In the article, E.J. described the set they used extensively in the Adirondacks to protect the trap from snowfall. They cut a hole through a hollow snag and placed the bait and concealed the trap on the inside. Dick and E.J. covered the trap with rotted wood. They covered the bait pen with evergreen boughs which helped with keeping snow out of the set. Snow rarely blew in enough to prevent the trap from working. The only thing that put the sets out of commission were blizzards.

Besides having two daughters, E.J. also had a son born in 1915 named Ansil. He died while picking blackberries on the Cunningham-Rennsalaer Falls Road in 1965. In an article titled "Our Indian Lake Trapline" in the March 1947 issue of The Trappers World, E.J. talks about his son trapping with him. He called him by his nickname of "Dutch" in the article.

Ansil Dailey, of Ogdensburg, and Miss Gladys Blume, of
Syracuse, fishing a branch of the Oswegatchie River at Edwards, New York.

These fox were caught by E.J. and Ansil during the 1937-1938 trapping season. In the October 1938 issue of Hunter Trader Trapper, an article titled "Learning about Foxes" by E.J. includes a photograph exactly like the one above except E.J. is in the photograph instead of Ansil.

Dick had a very short tenor as the Secretary-Manager of the American Trappers Protection Association (ATPA). This short tenor was the result of disagreements between E.J. and R.S. Oakes.

In the November 1936 issue of Fur Fish Game, E.J. wrote an article titled "True History of the American Trappers Association (ATA)". E.J. said he wanted to state the facts to ATA members because of a certain few distributing slanderous, misleading and untrue statements among members and officers. In the December 1936 issue of Fur Fish Game, E.J. announced in an article titled "Protection" that the ATA would now be called the ATPA. E.J. said that the ATPA would have the same leadership except Ray Bensley would serve as the acting Secretary-Manager. The Association would be based out of Columbus Ohio.

R. S. Oakes, who was the Secretary-Manager of ATA when both articles were published, did not agree with information provided by E.J. in either article. In the December 1936 issue of the North American Trapper which was the official publication of the ATA, Oakes wrote two scathing articles about E.J.

ATA letterhead.

He presented information provided by E.J. deemed incorrect by Oakes.

In the article titled "How True is True History", Oakes stated that E.J. tried to claim all the credit for the good that occurred in the ATA and blame others for the bad. Oakes made the statement that E.J. was replaced as the head of ATA and would not be connected with ATA after December 1, 1936.

In the article titled "Brother ATA Members", Oakes states that E.J. sent a member of the ATA a letter stating that the ATA had adopted a new name. Oakes stated that E.J.'s statement was false. Oakes thought the statement was designed to give E.J. an excuse for being removed from the ATA through adoption of a constitution and the election of officers.

Oakes said that ATA members should not send any dues to Columbus, Ohio and they should send no further membership dues to E.J. Oakes said that those who want to be members of ATA need to send their dues to Cedar City, Utah.

In the January 1937 issue of Fur Fish Game, Dick announced that he was asked to be the Secretary-Manager of the ATPA by E.J. Dick commented that he was opposed to the use of poison, to antitrapping legislation, to summer trapping, to killing furbearers on the pretense of being predatory animals and anything else detrimental to the best interests of trappers.

Dick envisioned the day when there would be motion pictures of wildlife and trapping life, annual conventions or rendezvous like the beaver trappers of the Rocky Mountains back in the heyday of the fur market, and competent legal representation in Washington D.C. and state capitols. Dick said he and E.J. had discussed the possibility of a trapping organization as far back as 1918.

In March of 1937, a new magazine called The Trapper was the official publication of the ATA. In that issue, Raymond Spears was noted as the President and R.S. Oakes was the Executive Secretary. There was no mention of Dick in the few The Trapper magazines which were published, nor were there any more articles about the ATA or ATPA in Fur Fish Game.

Dick, on the left, with E.J., in the center, and O.L. Butcher on the right.

Chapter 7. Walter A. Gibbs

From the fall of 1930 to December of 1933, Dick worked for Walter A. Gibbs and Son as advertising manager which included taking numerous photographs of traps and trappers using them. During this time, the family rented a house at 229 East Roland Road, Parkside, Pennsylvania, a suburb of Chester. They rented out the house in Red Bank. E.J. Dailey also worked for Gibbs over the same time period.

Gibbs Trap Factory.

In 1931, Dick along with Walter A. Gibbs accompanied a couple of Pennsylvania Game Wardens, Jess Hassinger and Leroy Jones, to trap nuisance beaver. Although their numbers had been decreased immensely, both New York and Pennsylvania had worked hard to re-establish the beaver. Gibbs was along because they were utilizing the Gibbs "Catch Alive" beaver trap and he wanted to view how well it worked in the field. They started at Schuylkill Haven.

At the first stop, the Game Wardens decided to try and capture the lone beaver by hand. After tearing out the lower dam, the beaver was spotted when the rapidly lowering water level below the main upper dam was no longer able to hide the bulky beaver. A half dozen farmers and boys in the area joined in the search. Finally, the beaver was cornered in a pocket in the creek. Jess Hassinger captured the beaver by hand and put it in a sack without injury to himself or the beaver. The beaver was transferred to a cage in a vehicle and the other dam was torn out.

Trapper with a selection of Gibbs traps.

The next area was in the mountains west of Mifflinburg. Another Game Warden, Miles Reeder, joined the group. The first stop was at a dam blocking a trout stream. Two Gibbs "Catch Alive" beaver traps were set here.

163

Dick sitting on a beaver lodge in Pennsylvania.

At the next area, the group found the lodge. They tore the dam out and waited by the entrance of the lodge with burlap bags to catch the beaver as it came out to investigate the falling water. No beaver came out, so they thoroughly searched the area, but were unable to find it.

They set four Gibbs "Catch Alive" beaver traps. The next day, the first two traps held a beaver. Both were alive, but one died later. The dead beaver was shipped to a Pittsburgh institute to be mounted. The other two traps each held a beaver as well. The next day one more beaver was caught and all the beaver dams were torn out.

The Gibbs "Catch Alive" beaver traps worked as designed with all the beaver caught alive. The one that died was young one and probably became overstressed from being in the trap.

Due to the Great Depression, Dick lost his job with Gibbs. Dick had also done some speculating in the stock market and had lost money when the depression hit. The family moved back to the house in Red Bank.

This photograph of Inez was taken near Chester, Pennsylvania.

Trapper setting out a Gibbs trap.

Dick wrote the following on the back of this photograph. "A misty morning on a Maryland muskrat marsh. W.A. Gibbs, famous maker of "Two Trigger" killer traps, is seen tending a line of experimental traps."

A misty morning on a Maryland muskrat marsh W.A. Gibbs; famous maker of "Two Trigger" killer traps is seen tending a line of experimental traps.

Photo by Dick Wood
Chattanooga, Tenn.

Chapter 8. Hunting

The cabin at Duck Hole was also used as a deer hunting headquarters. The person on the far right is E.J. Dailey. This is one of the few photographs where he is not wearing a hat. Photograph was used in the article titled "Afoot in Deer Country" in the November 1921 issue of Fur News and Outdoor World.

Dick's first hunts were in pursuit of squirrels in hickory trees. In the fall when the squirrels started to work the nuts, he would get his grandfather's old muzzleloader and get to the trees early in the morning. At the time, Dick was too young to hold up the long-barreled gun. He cut forked sticks to hold up the barrel of the gun. Dick usually hid in bushes near a tree. The squirrels had hidden themselves during Dick's approach, but after he was hidden, the squirrels would be back chattering and running from branch to branch. Dick dropped many squirrels using the cap and ball muzzleloader, but he wished he had a rifle that did not consume so much time to reload. Dick knew he could have gotten many more squirrels if he had a modern rifle.

Later in life, Dick had a varied collection of firearms. He had a Curtis cap and ball squirrel muzzle loading rifle which he used in the mountains of Virginia, a .303 Savage 26-inch barrel rifle, a .22 lever-action Marlin rifle, a 12-gauge Field Grade L. C. Smith shotgun, a .22 Colt automatic pistol and a .38 Colt officer pistol. Dick thought that a .30-30 was the best all around gun.

When Dick began to trap, he never carried a gun. He learned he could shoot additional game that was not caught in his traps. He started carrying the .303 Savage and the .22 Colt pistol. Game continued to escape because he could not shoot straight. Dick said he corrected this.

Dick killed more deer with the .22 Colt pistol than the .303 Savage, so he stopped carrying the eight pound Savage. Dick started in the morning with the Savage and the Colt in his belt. By noon, the Savage was cached in a hollow tree. During the fall of 1919, Dick shot a running deer with his .22 Colt pistol.

Dick thought that an accurate shooter did not need a caliber larger than a .25-20 and it was large enough for game up to black bear. Dick thought he could kill a black bear with his .22 Colt pistol. He commented it would take close firing of more than one shot in the right spot. In August of 1920, Dick said he intended to prove it soon.

Dick hunted with the intension of getting close enough to kill with one shot. Dick had been accused of being more of a hunter that a trapper. He thought there was some truth in that because he had been successful with small calibers.

The .22 lever action Marlin rifle was one of Dick's pet firearms. He used it mostly for sport after squirrels, rabbits and grouse. His Marlin was equipped with Marble's peep sight and a bead front sight. Dick could hit anything dead center with it. The rifle had at least one buck to its credit. It was a great, bait and trapping gun.

Dick preferred rifles, but had a 12-gauge shotgun. The right barrel was modified for birds, rabbits and squirrels. The left barrel was choked for ducks and crows. He never used it on deer or fox.

The Curtis rifle was homemade and always stayed in Virginia. It was a .28 caliber and the stock was curled maple. Dick hunted with it daily while a teenager. He learned to quickly reload it and molded bullets at night.

Dick's favorite type of hunting was for ducks especially while he floated down a river or creek. The limit then was ten ducks. He shot his first ducks, Mallards, from the eddies and sloughs of Pond Creek in Tennessee.

In the fall of 1918 between trapping activities, Dick hunted deer with Bill Wood at Shallow Lake northwest of Racquette Lake in the Adirondacks. They were after a deer that had been named Dare Buck of Hell Hole. Up to this time, the biggest deer Dick had harvested was spike bucks. Dare Buck was a twelve point monster and Hell Hole was a thick swamp which provided plenty of hiding opportunities. This swamp was located on the northeast corner of Shallow Lake. One advantage the hunters had was being able to track the deer in the snow.

Dick had an opportunity to shoot at Dare Buck, but the deer had quickly vacated the area. Bill told Dick to take the shot the next time he got it. Dick was harvested an eight pointer and Bill had gotten a spike deer.

On the last day of season, Dick and Bill's only focus was getting Dare Buck. Dick picked up the deer's tracks and was following it through some of the thickest cover in the swamp. He found it hard to believe that the deer went through some of the cover because of its antlers, but the tracks did not lie.

Dick on the South Chickamauga Creek.

Holdridge Greene, Triumph Trap Company employee and member of Dick's annual deer hunting group, designed this "Hunter's Jinrikisha" utilizing a motorcycle wheel and supporting material.

Dick said he had a determination that, once started, would carry him through purgatory. His habit of never turning back on a trail was acquired when he trapped as a lad and it stuck with him through all his outdoor experiences.

The buck left the swamp and walked along a stream. Dick found him on the ice in the middle of the stream and prepared to fire. Dick drew a bead on the buck and silently slid the safety back. Although he did not hear anything, the buck did. It immediately bolted and broke through the ice. The buck struggled for survival in the cold water.

Dick drew a bead on it again but dropped his gun to his side. A teacher in school had once taught him to never strike when the other person is down, and that principle stuck with Dick. If he had a means of helping the buck, he would have attempted it. Dick did not, without putting his own safety in danger, so all he could do was watch the buck fight for its life.

Soon the buck reached shore and, with great difficulty, climb the steep bank. The fight for life had exhausted the deer. Dick raised his gun again, but lowered it one last time. After watching such a gallant fight for life, he could not kill the buck.

Dick returned to camp and was questioned by Bill about whether he had seen the deer. Dick said that he did and had several opportunities to shoot, but explained what he had seen. Bill said he would have taken the shot.

Bill carried a 30-30 around camp. Dick said it was rustier than the box stove in Bill's camp. It had a broken stock which was held together by snare copper. Half the time, the 30-30 was cached in a damp hollow tree or log.

When going to town, Bill always cached it outside of civilization until his return. Bill did not want to be carrying a gun when he was drunk. Although the gun had not seen a cleaning rag and oil for a while, Dick was curious how many deer it had taken.

In 1920, Dick hunted deer in the Upper Peninsula of Michigan. This photo was taken at one of Rolland Ames' cabins.

In November of 1931, Dick shot a black bear in Potter County, Pennsylvania. He hunted with Byron Cottrell and others at Byron's place in Harrison Valley. Dick arrived at the Cottrell farm house after dark and was greeted at the door by Mrs. Cottrell. She introduced Dick to the group of sportsman around the table. Byron came forward to shake hands and introduced Frank Clark, an old trapper and guide. They spent the next hour smoking and getting acquainted.

The next day, they started hunting around Johnson Brook. Dick was stationed at a stand along with others. Three drivers were working their way towards his location, pushing deer in front of them. Dick sighted a deer with antlers and fired three shots. Two shots hit the deer and Dick marked the location where the deer was last seen.

Dick with his Potter County, Pennsylvania black bear.

Dick found a large eight point buck at the location. He noticed it was missing one eye, but was pleased that he now had a head. Another hunter had shot a nice doe and all the hunters helped get the deer out of the woods.

The next day was the last day of season and a large drive was planned for the afternoon. Dick already had his deer and was not needed as a driver so he was on a ridge sitting, in the open, smoking and watching the mountain.

Dick saw five deer heading for one of the hunters. The hunter opened up and fired eighteen shots. He killed one buck with a nice rack.

Dick made the bear into a rug which his grandchildren enjoyed. Dick's granddaughter on the bear rug in Red Bank in 1954.

Fifteen minutes after the shooting stopped, Dick was still watching the mountain top for the drivers to come into view and signal the end of the drive. Dick's eyes were drawn to a black object coming out of the denser woods. At eight hundred yards, he realized it was a black bear and it was coming straight at him. Dick stood up in the open and waited.

At about three hundred yards, the bear stopped, looked back over its trail, and listened. The bear started again at tremendous speed. Dick was amazed how fast the bear came sliding down the mountain side. The bear stopped at two hundred yards on the opposite side of a ravine.

Aware that if the bear would turn up or go down the bottom of the ravine, he would not get a shot, so Dick shot at the bear. The bullet hit behind the bear. It went down into the ravine and out of sight.

Suddenly, the bear popped over the rim of the ravine sixty feet away and, at a gallop, headed directly toward Dick. He threw the rifle to his shoulder and shot. The bullet hit the bear in the neck and ranged downward breaking a fore leg. The bear flipped over on its back, rolled against a bush, got back on its feet and started down the hill over its back trail. Dick emptied his gun at the vanishing bear. The bear was found dead in a nearby ravine. His hunting partners dubbed him "Dick, the Bear Killer".

174

Reverend Fred D. Watson admiring a 15 inch Rainbow trout taken on a fly in Santeetlah Creek in the North Carolina Smoky Mountains. Fred was also an accomplished hunter.

In the fall of 1932, Dick hunted duck on the Tennessee River with Reverend Fred D. Watson. They floated between Dayton and Chattanooga. This was four years before the Chickamauga Dam was built changing the river in that area forever.

Dick looked for the combination of cold weather and high water. The cold weather brings the ducks and high water puts the river at a level where the hunter can approach within shooting distance. If it is a calm, sunny day and low river level, the ducks congregate in flocks and stay out in the broad, open water. If it is cold and the water level is high, the ducks are forced close to the banks and the hunter has a chance of drifting down on them.

Fred's Buick was packed for a two day trip with Dick's two person cruiser boat strapped to the top. They picked up a third person to drive the car back after dropping them off.

Dick and Fred stopped at a favorite restaurant in Dayton just as it was getting dark. They ate and enjoyed cigars. After another half an hour drive, they unloaded at the Washington Ferry. The ferryman came to meet them with an invitation to warm themselves by the fire. Since it was late, Dick and Fred asked if they could sleep on his porch in their sleeping bags instead of setting up camp. The ferryman said they could sleep in the cabin, but Dick and the parson declined because they wanted to toughen themselves up for sleeping outside.

In the morning, the boat was portaged to the ferry and they had it loaded with their equipment after a couple of trips. An outboard motor was brought on the trip. Although not necessary, it is a nice convenience to have on a big river. The motor makes it easier to pick up dead ducks and move from one side of the river to the other with the high water. The motor also makes it easier to get to shore if there is a storm.

As the sun rose, Dick and Fred shoved off and headed for the opposite bank. By the time they were in the middle of the river, it had started to snow and the wind speed had increased. Small white cap waves started hitting the boat.

As they approached the south bank, the water was calmer and they were protected from the wind. Dick shut off the motor and used a paddle to steer. Fred was up on the front of the boat.

They rounded the first bend and did not see anything. They were in the best two miles of duck water between Dayton and Chattanooga. Further down the river, two mallards got up but were quickly out of range before either could shoot.

Dick and Fred floated by the mouths of two creeks where they often shot ducks, but none where there. Dick turned the motor on and pushed toward the opposite bank. Six mallards got up but they were too far out for a shot. They continued until noon.

Dick cooking after a duck hunt.

Dick and Fred pulled into a creek to eat lunch. The snow had barely whitened the ground, as it melted fast. As they continued, flurries punctuated the entire afternoon. They drifted down the river for miles without firing their guns.

Dick and Fred camped early that night. They had been content to camp in the open, but with the snow, looked for a farmer's shed. They found one on an island. A supply of corn cobs was used for the fire. The sleeping bags were spread on the planked part of the floor. The loosely planked walls provided some protection from the wind and snow.

The next morning four inches of snow met them as they looked out of the shed. There was no wind and it was clear. Dick thought that the mallards would be sunning themselves against the north bank.

Dick and Fred repacked the boat and headed downstream. About a quarter mile downstream, a flock of twenty to thirty mallards got up about a hundred yards away.

They floated a few miles and Fred heard ducks. He quietly let Dick know to be careful coming around the next bend. Six pintails got up not over thirty yards away. Dick and Fred shot three of the six.

Dick and Fred ate lunch on a drift pile on the river bank so they did not have to stand in the snow and mud. After lunch, they continued downstream with Dick in the front of the boat and Fred steering. Dick saw a lone goose standing on a sandbar about a half mile down river.

Added camouflage allowed Dick to get within 60 yards of a goose for a killing shot. For this photograph, Fred demonstrated how Dick looked when he shot.

The duck hunter on the Tennessee River seldom gets a shot at a goose. Dick wanted to sneak as close as possible before shooting so he and Fred piled vegetation on the front of the boat as camouflage. At about sixty yards, the goose took off. Dick sent two loads of No. 2s after the bird. A mile down river, Dick found the goose, dead and lodged against a drift pile.

The waterfowl that Dick and Fred shot.

Dick and Fred got three more ducks as they continued to drift downstream. They were about to call it quits when another goose got up about thirty yards from the boat. Fred raised his gun and fired. The neck shot dropped the goose.

One of Jack Miner's leg bands was on the goose. Fred wrote the conservationist about killing the goose and gave him the number. The band became one of Fred's prized possessions.

Dick and Fred stayed friends for several years. In a July 3, 1963 letter from Dick to his grandson, Dick commented that Fred expected Dick to take him trout fishing the next week, but due to a recent rain, they would have to wait for better weather.

This photograph was used in the May 1952 issue of Muzzle Blasts magazine distributed by the National Muzzle Loading Rifle Association.

Dick was a member of the National Muzzle Loading Rifle Association. He owned a .32 caliber percussion rifle which was made by Lester Smith of Johnson City, Tennessee. The stock was wild cherry and the rifle only weighed six and a half pounds. It was a squirrel hunter's dream. The powder horn was also made by Lester Smith. The tooled leather bag was purchased from Bropar of

San Antonio, Texas. The sheath knife was handmade in the shop of W. R. Randall of Orlando, Florida. The revolver was a Smith and Wesson .22-32 Target. The knife sheath and holster was by Heiser of Denver. The raccoon skin cap was courtesy of Pioneer Bank of Chattanooga.

Pat Sedlak took this photograph of Dick with his prized Lester Smith rifle.

Chapter 9. Fishing

Dick named this photo "Anglers Three". Tallest to shortest is Ross Hart, William Homer Hart and Brodie Hart. They are three of Dick's first cousins from Belle's brother, Jim Hart. William Homer Hart was also on the Gripping the Dollars booklet cover.

Dick started fishing in his teens using a bent pin as a hook. He played hooky on Sundays and fished most of the streams of east Tennessee. Dick went barefoot to the waterway and cut willow poles to use as fishing rods. He rigged them with stout cord and secured the end of the pole in the bank while he sat with his back to a tree waiting for a bite. When time allowed, Dick cut fishing poles out of the cane breaks. He selected long, straight canes and cured them before using. Dick dreamed of owning a bamboo rod and nickel reel like his father. He used a willow switch with a fork on the end as a stringer.

Dick titled this photograph "Life Begins at Seven". The boy on the left is using a forked stick as a stringer. Photograph taken at the West Buffalo Log Dam near Santeetlah Lake, North Carolina.

Dick caught his first bass in Pond Creek. He was sitting on a bridge across the creek using angle worms as bait. It was getting dark on that June day. Suddenly, the fish started biting and he caught several suckers and perch weighing from a quarter to a half pound. Dick's bobber was pulled under the water surface a greater distance than before. He set the hook and the tip of his cane pole bent below the surface of the water. After a short fight, Dick brought the fish onto the bridge. The hook broke and the fish fell right on the edge of the bridge. Dick grabbed it with both hands. He quickly headed home to exhibit his catch. His first bass was a smallmouth weighing about three pounds.

Dick called the black bass the universal fish being the most widely distributed and the most sought after sport fish. Dick refers to a quote from Dr. Henshall who he considered the foremost bass authority of the time. The quote was "Inch for inch and pound for pound, the black bass is the gamiest fish that swims."

Dick took largemouth bass from Florida lakes and smallmouth bass from Midwestern streams. He got the biggest enjoyment from playing a musky on a bass rod or fighting a barracuda on a 6 ounce bamboo tip. He realized that trout and bass were the country's greatest game fish and most of his trips were in pursuit of those fish.

After moving back to the Holston River area, Dick found that there was excellent bass fishing in the North Fork of the Holston River. Unfortunately on December 25 of 1924, an Alkali Plant Dam owned by Mathieson Alkali Works in Saltville, Virginia failed. The dam failed without warning and the waste material stored by the dam washed down the North Fork of the Holston River. Several houses were washed away and the final death count was 19 with some bodies being found six miles away from the dam. In his February 1925 article in Outing titled "Winter Touring the Adirondacks", Dick comments that any fishing possibilities in the Holston River had been killed deader than a door nail. The river did eventually recover.

Dick's early twenties were spent fishing in central New York lakes for walleye, northern pike and bass while working for the Triumph Trap Company. One of Dick's favorite places to fish while he lived in Oneida was Oneida Lake specifically off the pier at Sylvan Beach. Dick commented that this was a very popular inland resort with heavy summer traffic. He wondered why the dirt road leading to the resort had not been improved to a good highway. He concluded that it was because the mechanics at the garages wanted the business. The game fish in the lake included bass, walleye, northern pike, perch and panfish.

Dick took up dry fly fishing under the tutelage of Willard Spenser Jr. of Ohio who was one of the leading experts in the country. After that, he seldom fished wet flies.

Beulah cleaning fish at Oneida Lake.

The pier at Sylvan Beach, Oneida Lake. This photograph was used in the article titled "The Pier Patrol" in the September 1919 issue of Hunter Trader Trapper.

Dick said the sport in trout fishing was derived from the use of artificial flies. When the correct fly is used and properly fished, it is as effective as live bait. The art lies in being able to imitate the natural fly that composes the food of the trout.

In the spring of 1919, Dick fished the Cowasselon River in central New York. He learned artificial baits were not as effective as live bait before the middle of May. Dick did not catch anything with his artificial lures. He said he had the satisfaction of wetting his line and gazing upon the beautifully speckled side of a trout in another fellow's creel.

On May 25 of 1921, Dick went deep sea fishing off the New Jersey coast on a boat named Whitby. The boat had railings around the entire edge and each fisherman held their rods as they trolled. The trip cost $2.50 for the entire day with bait which was clams.

The deep-sea fishing boat whistled as it headed out of the bay. It took an hour to get to the Banks. The boat passed the wreck of the Princess Anne. On February 7, 1920, the Princess Anne ran aground off Long Island.

The boat continued down the coast past Sea Brighton and came to anchor over rocks. A deckhand distributed clams to each fisherman. Many baited hooks

Dick fishing the Cowasselon River in central New York.

hit the water as soon as the anchor did. Almost immediately, everyone started catching fish except for Dick. Looking down the side of the boat, Dick could see a dozen fish swinging in the air as they were hauled aboard.

Dick got ready to snap a photograph when something grabbed his bait. He dropped the camera. The time was around 9:00 am and for more than an hour the fish were readily biting. Toward noon, they stopped. This trip resulted in twenty-eight sea bass. The fisherman also caught hake, ling and whiting.

Several blowfish were caught. Once these fish were touched, they would swell up and look like a balloon. They also make a hissing noise. Every fisherman threw these fish back.

On the way in, the fishermen started cleaning their fish on the deck. Those who had more than they wanted, raffled them off.

Dick did not enjoy this type of fishing. He noted that there was a rough element that went on these fishing boats. The sight and smell of hundreds of fish being cleaned on the deck, the hot broiling sun, the curses of the rough necks, the drinking of rotgut, and the "everybody for themselves" and "the devil for all" aspect of the whole trip was disgusting. Dick said after this, if he could not find a cool brook with trout or a place to go surf fishing, he would stay home and fish in the bath tub.

In July of 1924, Dick fished Hoppins Lake with Harry Wootton from Utica, New York. Hoppins Lake is forty miles south of Utica. Dick arrived in Utica about sundown and called to Hoppins Lake to rent a boat.

Dick and Harry arrived at the boat rental and rowed to the opposite shore where the water was deeper. They landed on the edge of a woodland and cooked their meal over an open fire. Dick brought his .22 Colt automatic pistol and spent an hour target shooting.

After Dick and Harry ran out of ammunition, they started casting from the bank for bass. They immediately had strikes. They tired of fishing from shore and rowed out into the lake in hopes of catching some walleye. They used crayfish for bait, but the walleye were not biting very well.

The water was so clear, they could see the weeds growing on the bottom at a depth of ten to fifteen feet. Harry sent a crayfish down into an opening in the weeds and bet Dick a cigar he would catch at least a three pounder. Harry got a bite, set the hook and landed a four pound walleye.

Dick extended his alligator case containing one bit "As You Like Its" cigars. Harry said no thanks. He would wait until they were back in Utica and take a Corona.

Harry bet Dick another cigar that he would catch the next walleye. Harry let the crayfish settle again, got a strike and landed a two pound walleye.

Harry bet him again and caught another two pound walleye. Dick finally got a bite and landed a three pound walleye. Dick settled his cigar debt in Utica.

Dick purchased his trout flies from the Ernest H. Peckinpaugh Company in Chattanooga, Tennessee. He never tied his own. He requested Peckinpaugh tie orange bodied Tellico Nymphs for him. Dick used the Tellico Nymphs

This photograph was used on the cover of an E. H. Peckinpaugh Company Fishing Lure catalog.

extensively. They were not only effective in East Tennessee streams, where the lure originated, but also in trout streams in Maine, Montana, Washington, California, Alaska and Yukon where Dick had fished. He thought he had fished about every trout stream in Tennessee, but he never fished a trout stream in his home state of Virginia.

Dick fished frequently for trout with Ernest H. Peckinpaugh whom Dick referred to as "Peck". In June of 1925, Dick and Peck fished the Little River in the Smoky Mountains. Peck had written to a local guide by the name of Steve Owensby and let him know of the tentative time of their arrival. Peck asked if an automobile could get over the mountains. Steve wrote back that automobiles had gotten over the mountain range lying between the Little Pigeon and Little rivers. Dick and Peck decided to attempt that route rather than garage the car at Marysville and take the Little River Lumber Company train to Elkmont.

Most of the road from Chattanooga to Knoxville was oiled gravel except for ten miles of concrete north of Cleveland and there was a new highway between Lenoir City and Knoxville. At Knoxville, they ate lunch at a Gay Street restaurant and then headed for Sevierville.

The road between Knoxville and Sevierville was macadam. At Sevierville, the road narrowed to a mountain trail. As they climbed a mountain, Dick noted that the road would be very dangerous if they passed any cars. Because of limited visibility, Dick continued to honk the horn. Luckily, they did not meet any cars. There were only a couple of spots in eight miles of road where two cars could have passed. The road had some extremely steep grades and would be very dangerous in wet weather.

Dick and Peck arrived in Elkmont at 4:00 pm. They went to the lumber company commissary and spoke with employees who were sitting out front. They learned that Steve must be at home. It was a half mile from the village located on one spur of the railroad.

Dick and Peck stocked up on groceries and were directed to an area where they could camp. They followed a winding road, forded a stream and climbed a bank with their automobile. Dick guessed that the camping area was the most level ground within fifty miles.

Two boys stopped and were very interested in the headroom tent. It was very different from anything they had seen before. Peck offered the boys trout flies. While Dick and Peck set up the campsite, the boys, with the flies, caught three trout for the campers' dinner.

The next morning, the boys were at the camp at sunrise just as Dick and Peck were getting ready to fish. Peck gave the younger boy a shiny silver dollar in exchange for watching the campsite when they were fishing. The boy assured them that nothing would be taken either way, but he would watch it. The older boy was procured as a guide for the same sum. The older boy gave guidance on fishing spots both above and below the village.

Dick landed a three pound Rainbow trout and the boy told him that it was the largest trout taken near the village in more than a week. It was the first decent sized trout of the season for Dick.

Dick and Peck returned to camp for a lunch of trout. They offered trout to the boys but the they declined and left for home. The boys returned after eating lunch. They never tired of examining the bamboo rods, automatic reels and flies. Dick thought of his boyhood days when fishing tackle loomed before his eyes as the finest of the world's riches. Dick and Peck stayed in the shade of trees during the heat of the day.

That evening, Peck fished a couple of pools by a bridge upstream from the campsite as Dick prepared the evening meal. Peck returned to tell a tale of losing a large trout. Before breakfast, Peck was back at the pools. He caught a couple trout for their breakfast.

The sun was barely up when they left to find Steve. Dick and Peck had their tackle and lunches in a knapsack. They followed the old narrow lumbering road which paralleled the river until they came to Steve's cabin. Even at the early hour, Steve and his wife were working in the corn field behind their house.

Steve came out of the cornfield and said he had looked for them for a week. After introductions and passing out candy to the kids, the three were off to fish. They caught enough fish, at a spring in the river, to eat for lunch. The terrain got steeper, and the scenery got better. They caught more fish with the boys at their camp than with Steve.

Dick and Peck returned to camp and, as they came down the mountain, stopped at the bridge pools. Dick hooked a large trout, but it broke the line. The next morning, they left because the threatening rain would make it dangerous to traverse the mountain road.

In 1926, Dick and Peck fished for Rainbow trout on the Little Pigeon River in the Smoky Mountains. Dick drove his car down a narrow mud river road to reach the area. At one point, Dick went into what he thought was a bottomless mud hole. He stepped on the gas and luckily the tires took hold. There was soft mud up to the running boards

Dick wanted to turn the automobile around and go back but the road was not wide enough to do so. They continued through the quagmire and finally got to a point where the car was slowly climbing over huge, imbedded stones and tree roots in the road. They were an improvement over the mud holes.

Dick and Peck came to a dense thicket of rhododendron and laurel where little light reached the road. Dick turned a corner and saw three men coming down the road. Two had packsacks and one had a long barreled, muzzle loading rifle which was called a "hog rifle" in the mountain country. One of the men instantly jumped to the side of the road and returned without the packsack. The other man retained his packsack that had one heavy object in the end.

Because of the actions of the men, Dick slowed the vehicle and felt for the gun in the pocket of the car door. He did not know if the men were going to

Crossing the Little Pigeon River.

hold them up or were trying to ambush them, but he did not want to be unprepared to defend himself. As soon as the car stopped, the three men stopped and held a hasty conference in low tones. Peck thought Dick had made a mistake by stopping as it created suspicion.

   The man with the gun came forward as the other two men sat down to rest. Peck assumed the role of spokesman as Dick kept his hand by the gun. The man inquired about the reason Dick and Peck were so far up the road. Peck responded that they were going to fish for Rainbow trout in the Little Pigeon River and that they were strictly attending to their own business.

192

The photograph of Ernest H. Peckinpaugh in the Little Pigeon River area in the Great Smoky Mountains was used in the article titled "The Rainbows of Little Pigeon" in the November 1926 issue of National Sportsman.

The man said that was a good thing because further up the road in Hell's Cove on the headwaters there was a tough bunch. The man said they were much tougher than these three men may have looked. The man waved the other two men forward. As the other two men passed by, Dick could see the imprint of jug handles through the sacks.

The men said in a few miles the road started to ascend the mountain and from that point the road could not be traversed by car. At that location, there was a place where the car could be turned around. Dick and Peck continued down the narrow road.

The car was parked off to the side at the turn around point, so wagons could get by. Dick and Peck got all their fishing gear and food ready for a two day trip. Peck had assured Dick that no one in the hill country would steal from a stranger. To make sure, a sign was tied to the steering wheel. The sign said "To Whom It May Concern: This car belongs to my friend. We are up here fishing and not revenuing. PECK."

Peck had a reputation in the hill country, and his name attached to the car was the best insurance anyone could get. Dick and Peck later found out that an old hillsman and Civil War veteran had kept an eye on the vehicle. His house was visible from the road.

After a few minutes of hiking, they reached the Little Pigeon River. They started fishing and moved upstream. Dick started casting right away and Peck went up a couple hundred yards to fish. When Dick made it to where Peck started, Dick went a couple hundred yards upstream from Peck and started there. They fished all day like this.

Dick described himself as a fisherman by adoption. He had adopted the sport as an excuse to get outside and close to nature. Dick described Peck as a natural born fisherman. He was content to cast hour after hour without giving a thought as to whether he was catching fish or not. Peck's pleasure came from exact casts and precise techniques. Peck usually released legal trout and kept trout that were too injured to release, maximizing the number of hours fishing without violating any game laws.

At noon, Dick and Peck stopped and cooked their fish. A cabin was spotted near where they ate and Peck went to the house. Luckily, the lady was cooking corn cakes and he purchased a few. Dick and Peck napped after eating. Once awake, they continued upstream.

By 4:00 pm, they had climbed up the mountain quite a distance. The stream was now a series of waterfalls with a pool at the bottom of each where they fished. In many places, Dick and Peck had to leave the stream and follow the narrow wagon trail used by settlers living in the headwaters. The settlers used the wagon trail to transport lumber, corn and corn by-products to market at Gatlinburg in the valley far below.

About sunset, they came to the road's end. It ended at a small sawmill near the river. A mule path continued following the same course as the

Little Pigeon River in the Smoky Mountains.

river and they decided to stay on this trail until they came to a house, hopefully before dark.

Dick and Peck found a house and asked the woman if she knew where they could find lodging for the night. The woman said that they could stay with her and her husband. At the moment, her husband was out scouting the line. She said that the revenuers were after him. She asked if they were revenuers. Dick and Peck assured her that they were only there to fish.

The house was a log house on a bench of land overlooking the river. The couple had several youngsters who were all very interested in the strangers and their fishing equipment. Dick and Peck were welcome to the best that the settlers had.

In the morning, Dick and Peck continued up the mule trail. By 9:00 am, Dick and Peck had half a creel full of trout. The larger trout were on the lower sections of the river. The closer to the headwaters they got, the smaller, but more abundant, the trout were. About a mile or two above the cabin, they came to brook trout water. They had four more miles of stream, but could not fish it and expect to reach the car by night, so they started back down the mountain.

During the heat of the middle of the day when the trout were less likely to bite, Dick and Peck used the narrow trail to retrace their route back to the car. They made it to the car that night as it was getting dark. The next day they drove out.

In the summer of 1927, Dick explored usage of an automatic reel. The reel would automatically reel up slack line. If a fish pulled hard, the reel would allow line out against the tension of the spring. The tension increased as more line was pulled out.   The reel pulled the line in once the fish tired or swam toward the fisherman.

Dick never appreciated the worth of this reel for still fishing until he fished below the Hales Bar Dam across the Tennessee River not far from his home in Red Bank. Just below the dam and power house was excellent still fishing water. He was standing on an abutment thirty feet above the water. At first, Dick utilized long cane poles and braided linen line twice the length of the pole. He had plenty of hooks and sinkers as they frequently got caught in the rocks.

The real deep water was about fifteen feet from shore where fisherman with the longest poles caught the most fish. The best anglers used bobbers and threw out by the side of the powerhouse where the fish congregate to feed. With no reel, it was difficult to handle the long line required for this fishing.

The first fish hooked on his first trip there was a walleye. The fish put up a good fight and in a short amount of time had Dick's line wrapped in the lines of twelve other fishermen. This was not an uncommon occurrence. Dick did not receive any undue hardship from the other fishermen.

On his next trip there, he used an automatic reel with eighty yards of braded linen line. Dick pulled out just the right amount of line and cast to places that he could not reach before. In playing fish, the slack was taken up so quickly

196

that he never got tangled in the neighbors' lines. He used a twelve foot Japanese cane pole, with a reel seat above the handle, for fishing this location.

A seven and nine pound bass caught in the Ocala National Forest, Florida in 1928. This photograph was used in the August 1933 issue of Outdoor Life and on the cover of the July 1935 issue of Fur Fish Game.

Dick, Beulah and Inez camping at Big Lake in the Ocala National Forest in Florida.

In early 1928, Dick, Beulah and Inez travelled to Florida for the Acme Boat Company of Ohio and Coleman Company. During the trip, they camped and fished at Big Lake in the Ocala National Forest. On this trip, Dick and Beulah fished with the help of a young guide named Henry. They caught several bass and crappies while in that area.

One morning, Dick and Henry got up at daylight and, without taking time for breakfast, launched their boat. They paddled out beyond the weed fringe and around the lake shore for a quarter mile toward a point of land. Off this point, they had found that the bottom dropped quickly toward deep water and the weed bank hung over, creating a shelter for the crappies.

Dick dropped a lure down ten feet and started to retrieve it. A crappie quickly hit the lure. Dick set the hook and landed a two pound crappie. Henry used live minnows for bait. He lost two baits for each fish landed.

After about an hour of fishing, the crappies quit biting. They paddled back to camp and cleaned the nine crappies they had caught for breakfast.

In February of 1928 while in Florida, Dick and Beulah fished for barracuda off Key Largo. Dick considered the barracuda a better fighter than a muskellunge and more dangerous than the shark. He thought barracuda struck terror in the hearts of lesser fish, including its own kind, and that large barracuda constituted a danger to humans.

Beulah landing a nine pound bass with help of Henry, their young guide. This photograph was used in the article titled "Big Bass of Ocklawaha" in the September 1930 issue of Hunter Trader Trapper.

Dick and Beulah fished with Ed Butters from the Key Inn. The cruiser was on a small bay on Key Largo. They traversed a wobbly wooden trestle to a dinghy being handled by Ed's helper. They took the dinghy out to the cruiser.

Neither Dick nor Beulah were accustomed to the tropical sunshine. Dick kept clothing on to protect his skin. Unfortunately, Beulah did not as she wore a bathing suit. She was in misery for several days from the sunburn even though she was plastered with Unguentine.

About a mile out, they threw out their lines. The helper steered, Ed trolled and Dick stood in the bow of the boat. A yell announced that a fish was on and a Spanish mackerel was gaffed insuring their dinner.

They did not catch any other fish until they reached the edge of the Gulf Stream. The cruiser zig-zagged over the reef for several miles. During that time, they hooked and gaffed a few grouper, the largest being thirty-five pounds.

It took several hours to locate the barracuda. They started deep trolling in the edge of the Gulf Stream and were rewarded with some strikes. Ed finally hooked one and played it close to the cruiser. He grabbed the line with gloved hands and swung the twenty pound fish into the boat. Ed was a 200 pound athlete. He tossed the fish into the cockpit where Dick was standing. The fish's great jaws opened and snapped perilously close to his legs. Dick nearly jumped overboard.

Dick hooked a large barracuda which took a half hour to land. Ed gaffed the fish and brought it aboard. The barracuda was four feet long and weighed thirty-five pounds. The group caught two more barracuda. One weighed fifteen pounds and the other, thirty.

They trolled all day and returned to the Inn at 4 pm. They had caught five barracudas, three grouper and one Spanish mackerel.

Dick had the head of a barracuda mounted and hung in his den. When asked why he only mounted the head, Dick said that was all he got in the boat because other barracuda ate the rest of the fish before it was landed.

In April of 1928, Dick fished for kingfish off the coast of West Palm Beach. He stopped at the Chamber of Commerce office and talked to Gerry Swinehart. Gerry called Captain Wilson and planned the fishing trip. Gerry said to meet him at that office at 9:00 am the next morning.

The next morning, Dick arrived at the office and got in Gerry's car. Gerry drove to the Brazilian Court Apartments in Palm Beach. The previous night, Gerry had met Samuel Ralphaelson. He was the author of "The Jazz Singer". Samuel said he wanted to go fishing as well.

The three arrived at the West Palm Beach Yacht Club. They took a Mathews "38" and the captain was Bert Hiscock. They headed up Lake Worth for the channel. The boat was detoured to pick up Bert's fishing outfit and a couple of helpers to bait hooks.

Bert was considered the final word on East Coast Florida fishing. He was free at all times with friendly, expert advice and a great source of information for the fishermen.

Dick in Ocala National Forest, Florida. This photograph was used in the article titled "Outdoor Sports on the Caravan Trail" in the October 1936 issue of the Trailer Caravan.

The cruiser made good speed and the four miles to the channel took only a short time. The wind was kicking up rough seas and they trolled just outside the entrance to the harbor.

Dick did not bring the correct type of fishing outfit so Bert loaned his outfit to him. Dick had only gotten out fifty feet of line when he got a healthy bite. After fighting the fish for twenty minutes, Dick brought a three foot kingfish up to the boat. The helpers landed the fish.

Gerry put together some refreshments. Dick passed the fishing outfit to the next in line so he could partake while getting some rest. Dick got out his camera and took photographs including some of Samuel fighting fish.

Boats at Tarpon Springs, Florida.

In June of 1936, Dick fished Santeetlah Lake in North Carolina with Ted Davis. Dick set up camp near Ted Davis' cabin on West Buffalo Creek, a tributary of Santeetlah Lake. Dick headed down to the old grist mill dam at sunrise. He quickly caught enough smallmouth bass for breakfast.

Chris Zahnd netting trout for Fred Davis in Meadow Branch, a tributary of North River, Cherokee National Forest, Tennessee. Photograph was used in a Carl Zeiss advertisement in 1940.

Dick returned to find Ted out on the front porch of his rustic cabin, stretching and enjoying the morning sun. Soon after noon they started out on the Santeetlah. Dick and Ted were accompanied by Carl, Ted's son, and one of his friends, Gurley. Ted had a new runabout powered with a 60 horsepower motor. They ended up catching six bream, over a pound each, and numerous bass.

Dick camping near Santeetlah Lake in North Carolina.

Dick made another fishing trip to Santeetlah Lake with Paul Wilbanks – a Red Bank hardware man, John Swope – a contractor, and Mr. Dement – a banker along with their families. Paul reserved furnished camps from Ingram, a druggist, from Robbinsville. Ingram owned four or five camps on the lake. They arrived in the afternoon just in time for evening fishing.

Paul caught the first bream weighing one pound. He ended up catching most of the fish while chiding the rest of the group as being greenhorns. However, Dick recalled that Paul did not waste much time paddling the boat either.

The next morning, Dick was awakened at 4:00 am by other anglers yelling to one another with total disregard for sleeping occupants of other camps. Dick commented that he preferred a snug lean-to in the Adirondacks or a cruisers' tent on the Minnesota-Canada border far from the maddening crowd. Paul was over shortly to let Dick know that breakfast was being served in the screened dinning porch of their camp.

The group was out on the lake early fishing the shoreline towards the dam. At 9:00 am, Ted Davis came down from his camp on West Buffalo to join the party and give a few demonstrations in fly-casting. Ted already had a stringer full of bream and bass. After seeing how well Ted did, the group changed from fishing with live bait to fly fishing.

In the fall of 1936 while on an advertising trip in Ontario for Covered Wagon Company of Detroit, Dick and Beulah fished in Panache Lake. Panache was one of the best smallmouth lakes in Ontario. It was located eleven miles south of the Transcontinental Highway. Dick commented that drivers towing trailers should swing wide on the curves on the Transcontinental Highway and honk the horn frequently on the winding single track roads off the highway. They arrived at dusk after a slow cautious trip over a narrow, meandering gravel road.

Dick and Beulah launching their canoe in Panache Lake in Ontario.

Dick and Beulah camped on a high, level spot overlooking the lake. They thought they had enough fresh water to last the duration of their stay, but found that the tank had spring a leak on the rough road from Whitefish. For several days, they relied on lake water which they collected after rowing a few hundred feet from shore.

Dick met Henry Hutchinson at the boat dock on day. Henry was a trapper and wolf hunter during the winter months. He owned Bonnieview Island out in the lake. He insisted that they lock up the trailer and stay on the island with him, his wife and two children.

The next morning Dick and John Weiss, a Chippewa guide, were at the island dock loading an outboard motor boat. A sixteen foot Peterborough canoe was towed behind as they headed out for the day. They went by fifteen miles of shoreline before they turned into an arm of the lake. The arm gradually necked down until they were in a channel just a little wider than the boat. The wild rice and other aquatic plants were so dense, that the motor was shut off and they poled through.

They came to a portage and the motor boat was tied up. John took the canoe and Dick carried the rest of the items. The portage was over a mile long and finally ended on the shore of a Shuffelt Lake.

The portage back from Shuffelt Lake.

Log bridge in Algoma Region of Ontario.

The rest of the bridge.

Dick and Canadian guide preparing to cook lake trout caught trolling the north shore of Lake Superior during the 1936 trip across Ontario for the Covered Wagon Company of Detroit.

The canoe was launched and they paddled to a small rocky island a few hundred yards from shore. Several smallmouth bass were caught weighing up to four pounds. They paddled to the island and the guide cooked the smaller fish for lunch. After lunch, they had a smoke and laid down in the shade for a nap.

Dick and John took the canoe back into the lake. The fish in the main part of the lake had quit biting. John headed the canoe towards the mainland and came to a rest over a deep blue pool near a rock bluff. Dick let out line in about fifteen feet of water. He felt a bite and set the hook. After ten minutes of fighting the fish, Dick brought it to the top of the water and saw it was a walleye about two feet long. They returned to the portage with nine large smallmouth bass and a walleye.

In the summer of 1939, Dick and Beulah made their annual trip to the Hiltons, Virginia. During their visit, Dick fished the North Fork of the Holston River for smallmouth bass. After breakfast, Dick, with his gear, took off in the old skiff. For a half mile below the bridge in front of his mother's house, the river was too deep to wade. In places, there were rocky bottoms and some rapids, that held bass, walleye and catfish.

This deep pool was where Dick learned to swim at the age of ten. Below the deep swimming pool, he saw a bass swimming upstream where the water swirled around submerged boulders. Dick made a cast close to the bank and let the lure sink before retrieving. Suddenly, he felt a tug on the line letting him know he had a bite. He thought he had a bass, but it turned out to be a blue catfish.

As Dick continued to fish, he caught a glimpse of a swirl of water at the edge of some drift wood. He made a cast within a few inches of the drift wood. There was a mighty splash and he set the hook. After Dick landed the largemouth bass, he found it weighed over two pounds.

Just below the highway bridge, Dick pulled up against the north bank and found a wall tent set up on a narrow shelf of level ground. A barefoot boy, with his overalls rolled up to his knees, stood in the doorway. Dick learned the boy, Charley Wagner, was the caretaker for the camp. The camp was visited on weekends by a group of sportsmen from the mining district beyond Big Stone Gap. Charley had nothing else to do but fish.

Dick asked Charlie to go fishing with him. Charlie agreed and they walked to the bridge. Dick watched from the bridge as Charlie fished below. He made a cast and his lure landed at the head of the pool. A bass hit the lure and Charlie set the hook. He fought the fish for a short time before it was lost.

They separated and fished different areas. Charlie returned with three bass on a forked stick. It was now past 10:00 am and the fish had quit biting, so they parted ways for the day.

This photograph of the old skiff was in Dick's first article in Fur News titled "Notes from Holston". This was in the March 1917 issue.

Photograph of Dick printed in the September 22, 1940 edition of the Chattanooga Times.

Dick gave fishing one more try in the afternoon. He fished in the pool below the bridge and caught a 3 pound 10 ounce smallmouth. It was the largest smallmouth he had caught on a fly rod in the North Fork. As Dick landed the fish, he noticed he had an audience. Charlie and a couple of his friends were watching from the top of the bridge.

Chris Zahnd and Bess Morgan, who started as models for Dick's photography, would get married. Bess' sister, Irene, was also a model for Dick.

In the 1940s, Dick fished the Tellico River region of the Smoky Mountains. He spent many days fishing with Chris Zahnd, Dwight Taylor, Cosby Darwin and others in the angling fraternity who made headquarters at the Zahnd cabin on the Tellico River.

This wooden dam marked the upper end of the stocked section of the Tellico River.

Chris and Bess had an annual custom of holding an open house party at their cabin for the trout fisherman. Dick considered the Smoky Mountains and other mountain regions of the southern highlands a never-ending source of inspiration and material.

An afternoon's catch of rainbow trout in the Tellico River, Cherokee National Forest, Smoky Mountains.
This photograph was used in the February 1937 issue of Fur Fish Game.

In the summer of 1952, Dick fished with County Judge E.W. Waldron and Emmett Gowen below Pickwick Landing Dam which formed Kentucky Lake near

Savannah, Tennessee. They used slices of carp, about the size of a man's hand, for bait. They caught a 45, 35, 22 and 18 pound blue catfish.

Dick's sister, Nellie, shared some of the same interests as Dick including fishing, hunting and horse riding.

In 1950, 1953 and in August of 1966; Dick fished the trout streams in Baxter State Park in north central Maine. During the 1953 trip, one of Dick's sisters, Nellie, and her husband, Loyd, flew their plane from St. Petersburg, Florida to join Dick and Beulah. In the summer of 1962, Nellie and Loyd perished when they crashed trying to fly over the Rocky Mountains. Dick took the death of his sister very hard.

Nellie's husband, J. Loyd Yonce. with a 5 ½ pound bass caught in Watts Bar Lake in Tennessee.

In 1966, Dick was joined on his Maine fishing trip by his grandson.

Ansil Dailey and Beulah fishing for bass near Cardinal, Ontario.

Ansil with a stringer of fish.

Dick and Beulah fished with Ansil Dailey on the St. Lawrence River by Cardinal, Ontario. They were mainly fishing for bass.

Dick had one all encompassing tip for fisherman. If the fisherman wants to catch fish, ask the barefoot boy with the cane pole or the commercial fisherman. If the fisherman wants fresh air and sport, ask the sporting goods clerk.

Dick with a 45 pound amberjack caught 35 miles off Mullet Key, Florida in the Gulf of Mexico in the spring of 1969.

Chapter 10. Articles and Books

Raymond Smiley Spears. Raymond's middle name was his mother's maiden name.

Although Dick published hundreds of articles, writing, or any desk work, was always challenging for him. He was always looking for an excuse to avoid it. The Sportsman's Digest offered him $500 to write a book on camping, but he turned it down. Dick could stay at a desk long enough to turn out an article, but not a book of great length. Raymond Spears once wrote a book length article called "The Mountain Sheriff" for a pulp magazine. Raymond did this in one sitting in Dick's den while on a visit from Inglewood, California. Dick was impressed with Raymond's ability to do this.

The early 1920's was the high point for Dick's articles relating to trapping and various phases of the fur trade. During this time, he contributed to thirty-eight different publications. Dick published a few booklets at this time including Traps and Tricks That Get Furs, Trapping as a Professional and Narratives of Trapping Life. Traps and Tricks That Get Furs was a general how-to trapping booklet titled similarly to the Trapping Tricks booklets that he designed for the Triumph Trap Company. Trapping as a Professional includes sections on trapping different parts of the country with a few articles from other outdoor writers. The Narratives of Trapping Life included articles about Dick in the Adirondacks which had already been printed in Fur News and Outdoor World. There were a few articles from other writers in that book as well.

In the November 1926 issue of National Sportsman, Dick was introduced to the readers in the article "Shake Hands with Dick Wood". It was noted that as of that issue, he had camped in 35 of the 48 states. The article noted that Dick was an encyclopedia of motor camping information. He would not sit in an office and peddle information by the type written page. Dick was a wonderer who was constantly on the move, be it north, south, east or west. He was always in the field testing new equipment and methods. Dick sought out new places which had not been reached by the average camper.

In late 1926, Dick sent a flyer to tent and camp equipment manufacturers announcing that he was working for National Sportsman and Hunting & Fishing magazines. He also was the editor for the Motor Camping Department. Dick wrote about the expanding opportunities for outdoor recreation because of the automobile, better roads, and America's growing consciousness of its beauties and recreational opportunities. Later he had a fishing series called Pools and Ripples. The readership for the two magazines was over 377,000 sportsmen.

Dick outlined his plans while working for the two magazines. His first duty was to make the reader an enthusiastic motor camper. Dick noted that the value of the prospective purchaser to the manufacturers was gauged by their enthusiasm in the sport. He acted as the connecting link between the manufacturer and the consumer. Dick impartially field tested equipment and wrote reviews for the practical outdoorsman. He commented that readers are often skeptical of manufacturer's claims but a report from an experienced outdoorsman would clinch a sale.

Dick was the Camera Editor for the National Sportsman as well as Hunting and Fishing. In 1939, Dick was noted as the editor of the

Last Under the Wire
Start Motor Camping with Dick Wood on Page 44

Sportsman's Camera in the National Sportsman. His title changed a little, but he did the same job.

Prior to 1927, Dick had contributed articles to The Country Gentleman, Hunter Trader Trapper, Motor Camper and Tourist, Fur Fish Game, True Western Stories, Western Story Magazine, Wild Game Stories, Outers' Recreation, Sportlife and Outing. In Outing, Dick was the editor of a department for automobile campers called Motor Trails and Camp Life. He had a question and answer section for motor camping questions called The Motorists Service Corner in Outings as well. Dick was the trapping editor for Farm and Fireside and a contributing editor for Motor Camper and Tourist. He was also on the editorial staff of Farm and Home.

In 1929, Dick wrote a trapping book called The Treasure Book. Although it included trapping instruction, it was mainly an advertising tool for Herskovits as their lure was mentioned in most of the articles. It included directions on how to ship furs to Herskovits and books for sale along with other trapping items. Ironically, the cover had a drawing of a man setting a trap with a V in the pan representing the Victor trap brand. Dick never worked for the Animal Trap Company which makes that brand of trap.

In the February 1930 issue of the Mid-West Sportsman, the magazine announced that Dick was the editor of the Angling Department and that the magazine was now a national magazine. Dick's first article for Mid-West Sportsman appeared in the March 1930 issue.

In the 1930 and 1932 editions of Who's Who among North American Authors, several pen names for Dick are noted including Le. De W. Watson, Lon Baker, Blayne Smith, Robert Wilson and Dick Dubois. Dick Dubois was used because "bois" is the French word for wood.

Although not listed in those books, Adirondack Dick was used to document the author of, at least, one article. E.J. Dailey referred to him as Adirondack Dick on occasions and Dick referred to himself as Adirondack Dick as well. It should be noted that E.J. would call himself Adirondack E.J. Dailey and Dick would refer to E.J. that way at times.

In the November 1930 issue of Sports Afield, Dick published an article titled "A Trapper's Close Call" under the pen name of Dick DuBois. In this article, he describes having to kill a bear that had emerged from a crevice while he was walking on a narrow path on the side of a mountain. Dick had originally heard the story from Tom Walthy, an Adirondacks guide, on the train to Lake Placid in October of 1919. The original story was in a previous article titled "Hairbreadth Escapes from Wild Animals". Dick utilized the bear story as the climatic ending to "A Trapper's Close Call" even though it did not happen to him.

From 1935 to 1940, Dick was on the editorial staff of several magazines. He was on the editorial staff of Sports Afield writing extensively on woodcraft, camping and trailer travel. Originally, he edited a department called Motor

Tom Wathly at the Duck Hole cabin. This photograph was used in the articles titled "Hairbreadth Escapes from Wild Animals" and "A Trapper's Close Call" in the November 1930 issue of Sports Afield.

Touring and Camping. The department name was later changed to Trailer Travel and Woodcraft.

Dick was the Sports Editor for Automobile and Trailer Travel magazine specifically focusing on hunting and fishing. He was the Outdoor Editor for the Outdoor Sports on the Caravan Trail section of the Trailer Caravan magazine. He edited the Outdoor Trails for the Sport and Health department in the Lone Ranger Magazine. Dick also edited the Woodsmen and Woodcraft section of the Star Western magazine.

224

Note the "V" on the pan of the trap.

A drawing made from this photograph was used at the top of each of Dick's articles published in the Lone Ranger magazine.

Richard K. (Dick) Wood

Well known authority on outdoor life and woodcraft

Drawing in the Lone Ranger magazine.

The photograph was heavily cropped and had color added before being used on the cover of the February 1937 issue of Fur Fish Game. It was taken in the Adirondack Mountains.

Dick made contributions to several other magazines and other publications including Physical Culture, Field and Stream, Outdoor Life, Modern Mechanix, Tours and Detours, American Motorists, Popular Science, Outdoor Recreation, Sportsman's Digest, Farm Journal, Comfort, Far West, Canadian Countryman, American Boy, Target, Classmate, and Farm, Stock and Home.

On April 13, 1939, Dick received a letter from P.K. Whipple who was the editor at Sports Afield. Whipple discussed the discontinuation of the camping department due to the size of the circulation of the magazine. Whipple also said they had plenty of photographs from a recent contest as Dick must have been asking if they wanted to buy any. The editor commented that the woodcraft material from Dick may be sold to Sports Afield in quantities. The editor also hoped that Dick would stay on to answer reader inquiries for a few months. The editor commented that Dick had been paid for quite a few issues in which Sports Afield did not include any of Dick's articles.

Published in 1941, Dick wrote a book titled Camp, Trail and Canoe which was one of a set of sixteen books making up the Outdoorsman Handbook Series. In this book, Dick stated that motor camping was not as popular as it was in the 1920s. He thought that the increased abundance of tourist camps, the advent of the trailer coaches, the change in the design of automobiles and the complexity of modern civilization had been unfavorable to motor camping. Another factor he thought affected the decrease was the untidy appearance of the average motor camper's car. Too many would-be campers improvised equipment from home stocks and tied articles all over the car.

Dick also edited a section called Outdoor Sports and Recreation for the Chattanooga News. Topics varied from photography to fishing and swimming to equipment. He also included articles about visiting specific areas.

In an August 1966 letter to E.T. Bales, who was the Sports Editor for the Chattanooga News, Dick was upset that Bales printed a letter from a gentleman with the last name of Bordwine. Dick states "In view of the fact that this was nothing but a nasty, vitriolic disrespectful tirade against me, I'm surprised you published the letter, especially since he is not listed in the telephone directory and listed in the Chattanooga Blue Book as a bad credit risk. He didn't mention a single constructive sentence about trout fishing, but lambasted me for writing the article. Aside from these remarks, I have no reply to your reader who obviously isn't a gentleman much less a sportsman."

Dick used paper with "Outdoor World Syndicate" as the letterhead for letters during the Great Depression. In a July 3, 1963 letter to his grandson, Dick uses an updated copy of the letterhead with "North Chattanooga, Tenn" crossed out and "The Great Depression Letterhead" typed above it. The wording on the left side had also been updated to show the experience gained since he first had the letterhead printed. The updated wording follows.

"Outdoor sports articles, stories, and photographs. Over 25 years experience in Outdoor Sports from the Height of Land to Key Largo; Maine to Western Plains. Specializing in fishing, hunting, boating, canoeing, camping, woodcraft and outdoor photography subjects. Former editor and advertising manager. Contributor to all leading outdoor sports magazines. Nationally recognized ace photographer, equipped for any job, black and white or color. Open for assignments. Large file of stock pictures for illustration, magazine covers and advertising copy. Write your requirements."

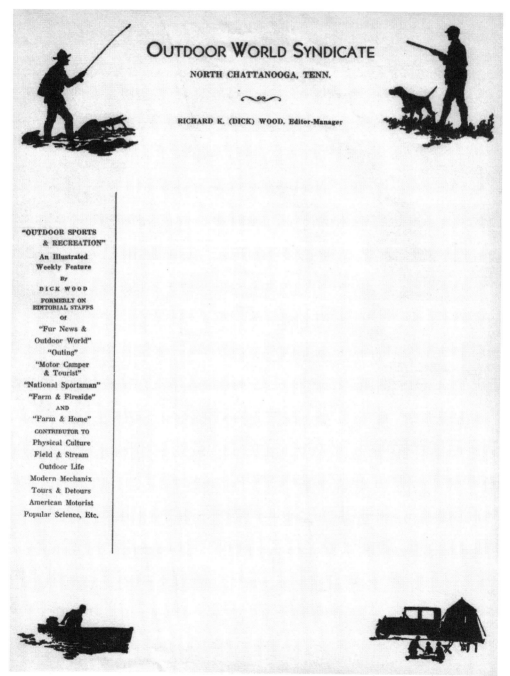

While living in Red Bank, Dick created the Outdoor World Syndicate where he was the editor and manager of Outdoor Sports and Recreation which was an illustrated weekly feature

Chapter 11. Photography and Advertising

Phone 7-3288   School and College Annuals

RICHARD K. WOOD
PHOTOGRAPHY

CAMERA EDITOR
NATIONAL SPORTSMAN   North Chattanooga
HUNTING AND FISHING   Tennessee

Around the age of fifteen, Dick was given a book about outdoor photography. He became increasingly interested in photography to the point that he saved up enough to buy a camera. Dick's first camera was a hand model of 4 x 5 or half-plate size. This was a folding camera with swing back, lateral front movement and focusing panel.

Dick always utilized a tripod and each photo was taken only after he had carefully arranged the composition and focused sharply. He thought the 4 x 5 was the best all around size for the advanced amateur to take contact prints large enough for publication without enlarging them. Dick began taking photographs as a hobby which immediately tied in with his love for nature and the outdoors.

Dick's first published photograph was in the November 1915 issue of All Outdoors. It was of two bluebirds and was titled "Don't Wink or Blink!" The caption for the photo was as follows. "This picture illuminates one method of getting photographs of young birds. The camera was set up and focused on the limb on which the birds are sitting; then the birds, two young bluebirds, were induced to pose in the required spot. Of course, this sounds easy, and it is, compared with the problem of photographing old birds, but even in this case there was a problem – there were four birds but only two could be induced to stay on the limb long enough for the picture."

The first of Dick's photographs used on the cover of a publication was in the May 1, 1917 issue of The Inland Farmer. The photo showed southern school girls who were members of a Canning Club demonstrating canning in tin cans and glass jars.

In 1922, Dick discussed the use of plates versus film. He stated he was done with plates based on his experiences as a field photographer. He said they were extremely breakable, heavy and bulky. Dick said these facts alone

Don't Wink or Blink. Dick's first published photograph in the November 1915 issue of All Outdoors.

Dick's first front page photograph. It was in the May 1, 1917 issue of The Inland Farmer.

outweighed the higher cost of the film. Portrait, cut and roll films turned out by a reliable company were satisfactory in quality for all ordinary work. The film possessed enough speed, orthochromatic qualities and obviating backing.

Dick frequently took photographs of company products before he had an agreement with them and then tried to sell the company his photographs. Advertising carried through in the trapping articles Dick wrote. While employed by the Triumph Trap Company, Dick's articles often included references to Triumph traps and while employed by Gibbs, Dick's articles included references to Gibbs traps. E.J. Dailey frequently referenced Triumph or Gibbs traps in his articles based on who he was working for at the time.

Dick took assignments from companies to tour with their products through different parts of North America. The photographs from these trips were used in advertising of their products. The product information was included in articles he wrote.

On June 15, 1927, Dick and Elmer Wade started on a two week canoe trip from the North Fork of the Holston River in Scott County, Virginia to Chattanooga. The vessel was a ten foot, sixty pound folding canvas boat which Dick named "Acme" for the company that manufactured it. Elmer was a Geology Professor from Ohio. He made the journey to make observations of the geology surrounding the river.

According to the article in the June 14, 1927 edition of the Knoxville News-Sentinel newspaper titled "Sportsman to Cross State in Flimsy Canvas Boat", Dick believed that the account of the trip would induce sportsman from many parts of the country to follow his trail. He also wanted to prove that East Tennessee streams and forested hills were on par with the famed Ozarks as a resort country. In reality, it was an advertising trip for Acme Canvas Boats. Dick wrote an advertisement booklet about the trip titled "River Cruising in an Acme".

In 1928, Dick, Beulah and Inez took a trip to Silver Springs, Florida for the Acme Boat Company of Ohio and Coleman Company. Dick met Ross Allen, the naturalist from the Silver Springs Reptile Institute, and used a photo with him to promote Acme boats and Coleman lanterns.

Dick with Ross Allen, the Silver Springs Naturalist.

The camper taken down and on the Indian River Highway in Florida.

234

Dick showing a Zeiss camera to a Seminole Chief while visiting Silver Springs, Florida in 1928.

Cree Indians in Manitoba, Canada.

235

This photograph of Dick and Beulah was used on the cover of the Spring 1932 L.L. Bean catalog. The photograph was taken by the Green River in Arkansas.

In 1934, Dick interviewed Walter M. Cline for an article in the Commercial Photographer magazine. Since he was in the photographic business to make money, Walter knew he had to give the public what they wanted. He said the public does not appreciate art for art's sake, but it does want artistic photographs of familiar scenes. People like to point to a photograph and say they have been there. They like old mills, mountain cabins, and anything that has an element of human interest in their photographs. An ordinary landscape will not sell.

Walter tried to connect his photographs with historical events or places with wide public interest. He said that a picture of Stone Mountain would sell while a picture of an even more striking landscape unknown to the public would not. Dick said that the information from Walter was a valuable tip to photographers. Dick also commented that too many people photograph what appeals to them instead of keeping the public, their market, in mind.

Dick was a staff editor for Crowell Publishing Company. While still employed with Crowell, he did free-lance writing and advertising work. Advertising turned him back to his first love of photography. It was taking its first great strides towards almost universal popularity with the perfection of the miniature camera and improvements in film and processing. The fundamental rule of advertising is that the layout be attractive and eye catching, especially the illustrations, and the popularity of the camera had enhanced the appeal of photographs for advertising.

Dick's work was both advertising and promotion. Creating advertisements, selling advertisements, promoting recreational pursuits and illustrating various types of activities developed his knowledge of appropriate advertising and illustrative photography.

Dick wrote "Photo Trapping Methods" after his time in the Adirondacks. This was a type written article on legal size paper with four plates containing four photographs each. The photographs show different types of trap sets and the article includes lure formulas from both Dick and E.J. Dailey.

Dick advertised this booklet for sale in the American Trapper in 1934. The advertisement stated that the secret of scent lures was alone worth the $1.00 price. It went on to say the booklet was endorsed by expert trappers as the most graphic methods yet produced for amateurs.

Dick took a photograph he titled "Going Fishing". Viewers saw a girl, boy and dog heading on a fishing trip. Unknown to its viewers, Inez was off to the left side trying to keep the dog inline. Of course, she was cut out of the picture when it was published.

Final "Going Fishing" photograph. A "C" with a circle around it was drawn on the photo in the lower left to represent that the photo was copyrighted. This photograph was cut down to just the boy and girl and used in the May 1934 issue of Esso Tours and Detours.

Original "Going Fishing" Photograph. The girl in the photo was Inez's first cousin, Doris Card, and the boy was Jackie Pitkin who is not related to the family.

This photograph of Dick and his sister, Nell, on the Holston was used in advertising for Evinrude Boat Motors in the November 1937 issue of Motor Boating.

Wolverine

1938 FIRST ANNUAL EXHIBITION OF Natural History Photography Sponsored By FRONTIERS A Magazine of Natural History

DAILEY'S
Animal Gland Lures

Best By Test

"DAILEY'S LURES" Attract All Fur Animals

My Lures are compounded from animal gland extracts and secretions, blended with other natural ingredients that appeal direct to the nature of the animal and will call them to your sets whether hungry or not, a thing common scents will not do, and the natural odors actually allays fear at the set. These lures have been on the market for over 15 years during which time sales have rapidly increased because the lure itself is the best advertisement I have. Like all good products there are now imitations, but trappers who want big catches should not experiment because the value of Dailey's lures has been proven in every State as well as Alaska, Canada and Mexico, and are used with success by both experts and amateurs and the same trappers buy year after year. These lures are not an expense but an investment that pays many times over on the trapline. Made in different formula for fox, coyote, muskrat, mink, beaver, skunk, weasel, 'coon, badger, otter, fisher, 'cats, civet, 'possum, wolverine and bear, also an odor eliminator and a trail lure. Price per one ounce bottle, enough for about 200 sets, $1; three bottles, $2.50; seven bottles, $5 postpaid with valuable set instructions, C.O.D. in U. S. if desired. Order direct from this Ad. I also stock the largest line of lure and scent ingredients in America, traps and other equipment.

E. J. DAILEY   **Ogdensburg, N. Y.**

241

In 1938, Dick won an award for a photograph of a wolverine. The award was given at the First Annual Exhibition of Natural History Photography. The event was sponsored by Frontiers magazine that covered natural history.

Dick also won a Kalart photography contest. He entered an evening flash shot of hunters returning from duck hunting. Kalart was a company that produced cameras and accessories.

Dick had a traveling platform constructed on the top of his automobile for high angle photography. It enabled a camera tripod to be placed solidly on top of the vehicle using a vacuum grip platform. The platform was used primarily for advertising photographs of boats and other outdoor recreational equipment. The goal was to show the structural plan or the use of outboard motors and other attachments.

In the June 1939 issue of Buick Forum, Dick discusses the platform to create uniquely angled shots "I had an order recently for a picture of an outdoor picnic dinner scene. Obviously, a right-angle view would have been commonplace. I got a fresh viewpoint by camera shooting from on top of the car. Again, I wanted an outdoor scene showing a girl's head among blossoms. The model stood on a step ladder to bring her head among the blossoms, while the right viewpoint was gained by working from the top of my car."

This photograph titled "Returning Hunters" won a Kalart photography contest.

Dick continues "This is my first Buick and, although it cost only little more than half what my last car cost, it is the best car I ever owned. When I get a rush assignment from an advertiser of a picture magazine, it takes me to the scene of action in a hurry. It gives me the much needed luggage space for my eight cameras and accessories."

Photo used in June 1939 issue of Buick Forum.

Chris Zahnd (upper left), Bess Morgan (lower right) and Irene Morgan (left of Bess) were frequent models for Dick's photography. This photograph was taken on Chickamauga Lake near Chattanooga, Tennessee.

Inez among the blossoms.

This photograph was used in an advertisement for Graflex Cameras in the June 26, 1939 issue of Life.

This photograph was used in a national Evinrude Boat Motor advertisement. It was taken at Ocoee Lake in southeast Tennessee.

Dick with cameras and equipment in 1940.

Dick had extensive knowledge of photographic equipment. In 1940, he had thirteen cameras. All of them were modern and different for a specific purpose. He had an extensive list of accessories including light meters; lighting equipment including floodlights, spotlights, flashlights, reflecting screens and diffusing screens to control light; filters to modify light conditions and colors to create moods and effects. Dick also had numerous auxiliary lenses for close or distant work, wide angle shots and landscape of portraiture shots.

The May 1940 issue of U.S. Camera, one of the foremost American journals of photography, listed Dick among the twenty-two leading illustrative photographers in the Unites States. He had covered special assignments for Life, Look and National Geographic magazines. Dick's photographs had been used by national advertisers including Standard Oil Company, General Motors, Evinrude Motors, Mans Corporation of Chicago, Folmer-Graflex Corporation and Carl Zeiss.

In the September 15, 1940 article of the Chattanooga Times titled "Meet Dick Wood, Chattanooga Photographer", the writer comments on Dick's slow drawling speech and notes that some of his friends say this is because he likes to taste his words. Dick believed it was because he thinks twice before he speaks. The writer believed this provided a true estimate of Dick as a man. He was careful, painstakingly methodical and studious when applying himself to any problem at hand.

Dick provided photographs and quotations for other advertisers including those selling cameras and fishing lures.

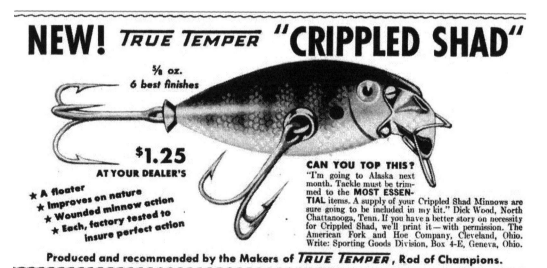

Advertisement in the June 1948 issue of Popular Science.

Dick also took school photos.

Standard Oil Company produced a brochure of the Scenic South in November of 1966. One of Dick's photos, three possums on a fence, was used in the brochure.

Dick wrote a note about the photograph. "While visiting a cousin, Ralph Hart, on a farm near Hiltons, VA., we heard the farm dog barking early one morning and discovered it had three possums treed on a rail fence, near a persimmon tree. Having a new Graflex camera to try out while the marsupials were intently watching the canine, I composed this animal portraiture."

Standard Oil Company Scenic South brochure in November of 1966.

Ralph Hart, Dick's cousin, trying to catch the three possums after they left the fence.

Bald River Falls photograph used in both the Dana Corporation and Scenic South fliers.

In 1966, Dick contributed a photograph of the Bald River Falls in Cherokee National Forest near Tellico Plains, Tennessee to a flier by the Dana Corporation. The flier advertised Perfect Circle Piston Rings.

Dick was photographed by some notable people. At the end of the Hunting Chapter in this book, there was a photograph taken by Pat Sedlak, an antique trap collector. He was also photographed by Maurice H. Decker who wrote and published many outdoor articles.

Dick and Beulah at Cape Coral, Florida in 1967. Photograph was taken by Maurice H. Decker.

Dick also contributed several photos for the July – August 1968 edition of the Scenic South. One photo was very similar to the Bald River Falls photograph used in the Dana Corporation flier.

Dick said photography was a complex mixture of art, science, chemistry and mechanics. Understanding these items, he developed a deep love for photography that made him a tireless study and willing to work for improvement. Although he had already sold numerous color pictures for magazine covers and advertising, Dick was deeply interested in advancing his expertise in color photography. It was still in its infancy. He thought color photography would advance quickly to be the main medium of advertising. Dick used his extensive knowledge of the outdoors, along with his knowledge of photographic equipment, to produce high quality photographs.

WEEKI WACHEE SPRING

Family of raccoons at Weeki Wachee Spring, Florida looks over a just-vacated picnic spot to see if any goodies were left.

Richard K. Wood

Page from the July-August 1968 Scenic South flier.

Dick getting ready to take a photograph.

255

Dick often typed or wrote information on the back of photographs. He also stamped the backs with where he lived at the time the photograph was made. The stamped locations of where he lived did not always line up with when the photograph was taken.

Chapter 12. Passions

Beulah and Inez

Besides his outdoor interests, Dick found passion in other areas including family, the Outdoor Writers Association of America and tobacco. Dick's greatest passion was Beulah whom he met at Warner Park in Chattanooga in early 1916.

When Dick included Beulah in his articles, he referred to her as the "Missus", including the quotation marks, or Mrs. Wood. Dick usually called Inez by her name except for a few occasions. In a motor camping article, Dick called her Miss Junior Camper. Although he had many pen names, Beulah only called him Richard and nieces and nephews called him Uncle Richard.

In an undated love letter, Dick expressed his feelings for Beulah. He discussed Beulah's comment that she was not like other girls. This comment probably focused on Dick being gone from home frequently and for long periods of time or his wife traveling with him. Other women did not like absent husbands. Beulah tried to convince Dick that his lifestyle would not bother her.

This photograph of Beulah was used in an advertisement for Beech Nut Peanut Butter in Field and Stream.

Miss Beulah Graham
North Chatta, Tenn

My Dear Miss Beulah,

It is needless, I suppose for me to say that it is a great pleasure to write you, since I must take your advice of the other night. Remember? However, I must say, it was an unlooked for opportunity that I should have the fortune of meeting, Friday, the most charming and fascinating girl that I have ever met – and it seems too good to be true that I now have the pleasure of writing her. It seems Friday is my lucky day and I sincerely hope that I shall never have occasion to change my mind.

I came back to Daisy Sunday in hopes of seeing you, and am now out in this "God forsaken" country. So because I can't see you, have you arrived home yet? And will the party on Walnut Street come off? I have made arrangements to be up here all week but, believe me, if I knew you cared a snap to see me, I'd wade through all this backwater to get there! Since it takes 2 days each way for a letter to go, it looks like you can't get word here in time. Had I known for sure that this party would come off, I would have been either in Hixson or Chatta now. However I'm living in hopes that Friday night shall not be the only opportunity that I will have of being with you.

Dear Miss Graham, you said that you did not like for me not to believe you but you can realize, I am sure, how hard it is for me to believe that I have at last, met one girl that is not like other girls! Whether you are like other girls or not, I must say, you are the only girl I ever met that so enchanted me with her charms that I would wade mud holes and climb clay banks! Ha! No wonder, who would not be enchanted by the sweet little country girl that sits over on the mountain side and makes love to the "man in the moon"! How I envy the man in the moon and how I pray and wish that the moon would never shine again until that night, when I can be by your side and look with envy upon the face of the "man in the moon", and on that night may the face disappear and shine no more! Then and not till then shall my sincere hopes for the future be accomplished.

I have heard songs of "Beulah Land", have read of fairies and dreamed of honey land, but it seems too good to be true that before my eyes has appeared the real girl that formed the "Dream Girl".

Dick was lucky to find a woman like Beulah who supported his trapping and other career interests. Who else would have put up with raising a child while he followed his career activities as a nomad at times? From living in tents after leaving New York City to traveling all over the country to test equipment and taking advertising photos, Beulah was the perfect match for Dick.

Beulah and Inez were often included in Dick's traveling plans most frequently in the warm season months. Sometimes they were left behind, more often in the cold season months. When Dick and Beulah traveled without Inez, they left her with Dick's mother, Belle, in Hiltons, Virginia. Inez enjoyed time with her Grandmother Wood and never made any complaints about her.

Beulah was very understanding of Dick being away from home for extended time periods or traveling with Dick and their daughter. Once they were settled, she had one rule - no alcohol allowed in the house. However, Dick kept spiked eggnog in the garage refrigerator for the holidays.

Inez and Beulah in automobile.

Dick showing Beulah how to shoot his hand gun.

Beulah's family photographed on November 30, 1919. Beulah, with Inez on her knee, in the lower left corner

Grandmother Belle Wood in Hiltons, Virginia..

Beulah holding a photograph of Dick in the Adirondacks.

Inez with squash in the garden.

Outdoor Writers Association of America

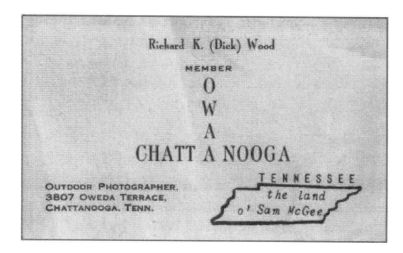

Dick was the last survivor from the list of names appearing on the original Bill of Organization of the Outdoor Writers Association of America (OWAA) at the 1927 Izaak Walton League of America meeting in Chicago. Although many called him a Charter member, Dick pointed out that he did not join the new association until the following year, even though his name was on the list. He always took great pleasure in his OWAA membership and enjoyed attending the conventions. In Dick's will, he left a bequest of $500 to the OWAA.

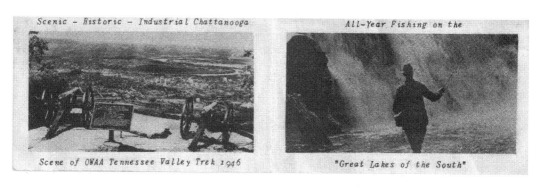

He actively participated in events including a tour of the Tennessee Valley in 1946 and an Alaska tour in 1947. Dick's frequent inclusion of the term "sourdough" to describe trappers came from his reading the book of poetry titled Songs of a Sourdough published in 1907 by Robert W. Service. The book included the poems titled The Cremation of Sam McGee and The Heart of the Sourdough.

Sam McGee was a fictional character, but the name came from a person named William Samuel McGee. The real McGee was a miner, teamster, sawmill operator and road builder.

The character McGee was from a fictional town in Tennessee named Plumtree. There is a town named Plumtree in North Carolina only a short distance away from the Tennessee border. The real McGee headed for the Klondike gold rush in 1898.

Dick visiting Sam McGee's Cabin in Whitehorse, Yukon Territory, during the OWAA Alaska Tour in 1947.

Jeff Anderson, from Ketchikan, Alaska, guided Dick to fishing spots on Wilson Lake.

During the Alaska trip, Dick fished for Cutthroat Trout on Wilson Lake by Ketchikan. The lake was only accessible by pontoon plane.

Jeff Anderson fishing in Wilson Lake.

In June of 1949, Dick and Beulah attended the Outdoor Writers' Convention in North Bay, Ontario. According to Dick, the conventions were like paid vacations with most meals being free, guides furnished for local trips and cocktail parties every night.

After attending this convention, Dick and Beulah traveled to Sudbury. They then contacted Nickelbelt Airways about flying them to Blue Mountain Lodge on Bell Lake. The flight was 20 minutes compared to an all-day trip by automobile and boat. They spent a week at the lodge fishing and taking wildlife photographs.

In June of 1968, Dick attended the Outdoor Writers' Convention at Callaway Gardens in Pine Mountain, Georgia. He was the oldest member to attend this gathering. He then paid a visit to the Okefenokee Swamp in southern Georgia before returning home on July 1st.

In Okeefenokee Swamp

In 1972, Dick felt he should resign from the OWAA. The Board of Directors, in recognition of Dick being the lone survivor from that organizational document, voted him a Life Membership that year. Dick was deeply pleased about receiving this honor and communicated with the OWAA headquarters annually thereafter.

J. Hammond Brown, President of the Outdoor Writers Association of America, with a nine pound trout taken near Anan Creek and the inland passage in Alaska in 1947.

Tobacco

One of Dick's partners opening a can of Velvet Smoking Tobacco. Dick referred to it as velvety Velvet.

As a lad, Dick was first exposed to smoking tobacco while tending to a curing house on an uncle's tobacco farm. He and another lad from the neighborhood were instructed to take care of the curing operations. They made their initial adventures into hand rolling and smoking tobacco. Dick said that one of the long hand rolled stogies would give them more kick than a quart of Canadian hard cider.

Years later, Dick and Bill Wood had caught a cross fox that showed silver fox possibilities. They wanted to get the fur out on a high market and made the trip without a toboggan. They were returning to their camp at Little Gull Lake from Matagami which was fifteen overland miles.

Dick and Bill utilized snowshoes and backpacks. They carried a few supply odds and ends and mail evenly distributed between their two packs. Within sight of their cabin, they crossed the Grassy River on a long slim spruce felled for that purpose. The water never froze in that area because the river was too swift.

Bill started to walk across and had released his arms from the packsack to cross the dangerous water. The pack hung over one shoulder and was easily released if he lost his balance. His right foot hit glare ice and it was impossible to keep his balance without releasing the backpack.

The pack hit the water and floated downstream, slowly sinking as water leaked inside. Bill sprang to the opposite bank. He luckily retained his snowshoes and rifle. He rushed downstream after the pack.

A short distance downstream, the water was frozen and any floating object was sucked under. Bill reached the ice ahead of the pack. He walked toward the middle of the stream where the water was swiftest. The ice held him near the bank, but he went through the thinner ice near the middle. Luckily, he grabbed the pack before it went under. The ice was not strong enough to hold his weight and he broke his way through the ice to the bank.

Dick thought he was crazy to take a chance like that so far from help and let Bill know. Bill let Dick know that the pack held all their tobacco and he did not intend to lose it so close to camp. During the next snow storm when they were holed up, he wanted to make sure they had tobacco to feed their pipes. Tobacco was utilized considerably during snowstorms when they stayed in the cabin all day with nothing else to do.

In August 1919, Dick rode with Bill Randall forty miles back to fish the Boreas. Bill drove with reckless abandon as he whipped around the hairpin curves with one hand on the wheel, quickly slowing to forty miles an hour and then speeding back up again. Dick commented that he thought he had pretty fair nerves and they were reinforced with a big chew of plain scrap tobacco. When Bill's driving was too much for his nerves, he would concentrate on the tobacco.

In 1920 while trapping around Republic, Michigan, Dick was running low on tobacco. He discovered "Edgeworth" in a cabin and called it an exquisite tobacco being extremely mild. Dick commented that he expected to cultivate its acquaintance further. He eagerly confiscated the two pipe fulls left in a can.

In the March 1921 issue of Fur News and Outdoor World, Dick discusses Edgeworth tobacco in "Trail Tested and Right". Even after trying Edgeworth the year before, Dick still thought that he smoked the only real tobacco that was ever cured - Velvet. Then he ran out. He took it for a week. He heard of an abandoned, unlocked hunters' camp a few miles away. E.J. Dailey suggested giving the place a once over for cached tobacco. E.J. said the owners were his friends and he would explain. That was how Dick gave Edgeworth a second, more thorough, try. Dick said the tobacco would please the most discriminating pipe smoker. He sent a carton of Edgeworth to the camp owner later.

In the same issue of Fur News and Outdoor World, Dick, in "Trappers' Equipment", describes a Life Saver Kit that trappers and hunters should carry with them. He had a rule that if the safety match box was partly or wholly emptied, it was immediately refilled. Dick discussed trappers having to go fireless at an ill time because they had used their reserve matches for lighting the pipe. Dick said it was better to go smokeless than fireless.

In the July 1921 issue of Fur News and Outdoor World, Dick discussed his favorite pipe in trail "Tested and Right". Dick's favorite pipe was a Maier with a nicotineless stem made in St. Charlestown, Maryland. Dick said the nearest he ever came to bunking with a mad man was in the Michigan Peninsula, when the trapper he was with broke his only pipe. The other trapper hiked out twenty miles to get another. Dick said he insured successful and pleasant trips by having an extra Maier along. He then goes into great detail describing the qualities of the Maier pipe.

In June of 1925, Dick and Peck were enroute to fish the Little River at Elkmont in the Smoky Mountains. Dick said that while enroute they talked trout fishing and consumed a package of good smoking tobacco. During the second evening, the mosquitoes had driven them into the shelter of the tent. They read, played cards and exchanged tales from past trouting trips. Dick commented that they kept their pipes glowing and doubted that a mosquito could have survived inside the tent had it squeezed through the bobbinet tent door.

Sadly, one of Dick's greatest passions had a part in his passing as he died from lung cancer.

Dick even kept his cigar when swimming.

Chapter 13. Odds and Ends

Travel

Dick and Beulah with an amphibian plane.

From 1947 to 1949, Dick flew over wilderness areas of the Rockies, Alaska, Yukon Territory and Ontario. Dick commented that the preferred method of travel in the wilderness areas was by amphibian plane due to limited road access. That was, if the person could afford it. If not, then it was by waterway.

Assistant Conservation Officer

Chattanooga, Tenn. (Hamilton) 3807 Oweda Terrace ·   Approved by Walter L. Martin

To All Who Shall See These Presents, Greeting:

KNOW YE, *That whereas, the State Director of Game and Fish of Tennessee is authorized and empowered to appoint Assistant Conservation Officers, under Section 2, Chapter 160, Acts of 1939.*

NOW THEREFORE, *I, R. G. Turner, State Director of Game and Fish, by virtue of the power and authority in me vested, do hereby appoint*

RICHARD K. WOOD

Assistant Conservation Officer, to enforce all Game and Fish laws that I, as State Director, could or ought to do.

Given under my hand and official seal this 29 *day of* April , 19 43

Game and Fish Director.

On April 29 of 1943, Dick was appointed an Assistant Conservation Officer for the State of Tennessee. R. G. Turner, the State Tennessee Director of Game and Fish, authorized Dick to enforce all game and fish laws in the state. This was approved by Walter L. Martin. There are no records showing Dick had any type of law enforcement training or that he ever used the authority to enforce any fish or game law.

The Museum of the Cherokee Indian

You are cordially invited
to be present
at the

Cherokee Indian Feast

Museum of the Cherokee Indian, Cherokee, North Carolina

Sunday, November 28, at Two P. M.

Wild Meats and Foods used only by the Indians
prepared by the Indian Women

Brief Addresses on Domestic Life of the
Ancient Cherokees

The courtesy of a reply by November 22 is requested.

On November 28, 1948, Dick attended the opening of the Museum of the Cherokee Indian in Cherokee, North Carolina. In the invitation, H.E. Wheeler, the director of the museum, requested that Dick bring his camera to take some photographs. Wheeler sent his friends a distinctive Christmas card each year. At the time of the opening, he did not have a camera and hoped Dick would be open to taking a photograph of a curious corner of the museum or something about the feast that would easily and economically produce a Christmas card. Wheeler said that if it did not work out, the important thing was that Dick was attending the opening.

One hundred twenty-five visitors from the old Cherokee Nation territory "returned to the blanket" for the event. The museum was founded by Samuel E. Beck. Moses Owl, a Cherokee chief, and his Pueblo wife served as guides for the visitors. They demonstrated and explained various instruments and articles in the museum.

The highlight of the event was a dramatization of a Cherokee marriage. The parents of the daughter hold a switch, over which the lovers must leap. If they fail to make the leap, they must wait another year. The height that the switch was held depends on whether or not the mother looked with favor on the suitor.

Retirement

Dick and Beulah with grandchildren in 1959.

In 1960, Dick retired and moved to Ringgold, Georgia, on the south side of Chattanooga. Dick retired "to go into the mowing and gardening business". His hobbies, through his life, were, first, trying to emulate Daniel Boone, then girls (until he got hooked) and, after retirement, it was trying to beat Wall Street. Dick had stocks before retirement and focused more energy on beating Wall Street with the additional free time.

In retirement, Dick handled a personal stock fund that included over sixty equities. He also oversaw a separate bond account, Beulah's account and advised two nephews and three friends on their accounts.

In a July 3, 1963 letter to his grandson, Dick encouraged his grandson to hang onto his stocks until the next "bull" market. Dick thought the next bull market would probably start in 1965. He thought the shares would sell for about $30 each. He commented that in 1961 he sold 100 S-R for over $30 each and sold 100 Adam's Exp. in 1962 for $30.50 per share. He commented that the high on American Motors had been around $32.50.

In the same letter, Dick discussed how it never pays to throw anything away until necessary especially with moving so much. In the letter, Dick had sent his grandson some tent patches. Dick had been searching for the patches for a

277

while and eventually found them in an old tool box. Dick also shared that a front wheel had fell off his riding mower. The only thing he had to put it back into working order was an old girdle buckle Dick had saved in a tool box.

In 1971, Dick thought about writing a how-to book for the investor, but never did. In a 1971 letter to Inez, Dick commented that the market had been up and down like a window curtain with the long-term trend uncertain. Dick said his best growth companies were Apco Oil, Neublein, Tootsie Roll and Weiboldt Stores. He suggested that Inez get a dime store book like his and start a chart on the stock list he gave her. Dick said she had much to learn about investing but he had an immense library on the subject that was available to her.

Before Dick died, Inez learned enough about the stock market to convince him to eliminate his margin accounts. They are more risk because he bought stocks on money borrowed from the broker. After Dick died, Inez took classes in investing in the stock market and managed her stocks.

House in Ringgold, Georgia.

Chapter 14. Legacy

Dick's legacy has no stronger ties than those to the Cold River area. This photograph was used on the cover of the December 1920 issue of Fur News and Outdoor World.

Dick passed on November 1, 1977 and Beulah passed on November 8, 1979. Dick and his family were always on the move. It was the foundation for his far-reaching legacy which positively impacted outdoor writing and photography.

Dick lived in a simpler time. It was both good and bad. For instance, sleeping in someone's shed without permission or arriving unannounced to a remote house was commonly done by Dick. In both cases, he was welcomed and given the best the owner had. On the other side, the road system was not developed, maps were lacking and driving long distances was an adventure itself.

His younger years provided the experience and a warehouse of memories which were used later in life as a base for many articles. Dick's first articles focused on trapping and his outdoor adventures in the Adirondacks. Later his focus was on motor camping and photography. Dick's interests were varied which was evident in the wide variety of topics he covered.

Dick wrote articles for at least seventy-seven different publications in his lifetime. He went full circle back to his first love of photography and made it into a career later in life. In retirement, Dick focused on his passions of the Outdoor Writers' Association of America, Beulah and Inez, and tobacco. He also had more time to try to beat Wall Street.

Dick foretold the future with four of his comments in this book. He discussed vintage pamphlets and books that were considered junk and discarded. Just a few years later, the material was considered a valuable record of a time that had passed and gone into history. Dick said the buckskin trapper would soon pass over the last long trail just like the buffalo, the passenger pigeon and the beaver. Dick envisioned the day when there would be motion pictures of wildlife and trapping life, annual conventions or rendezvous like the beaver trappers of the Rocky Mountains in the heyday of the fur market, and competent legal representation in Washington D.C. and state capitols. Although color photography was in its infancy, Dick thought color would advance quickly to be the main medium of advertising photography. To one degree or another, all his comments came true.

Dick's legacy is engrained in the articles he wrote, the pictures he took, the places he visited and the people he met during his life. To say he was gregarious is an understatement based on the number of names included in this book. And several people could not be identified from photographs!

Dick was a hardworking man who made an honest living by writing articles and taking pictures of the activities he truly enjoyed. Few people live life on their terms, Dick was one who did.

This photograph was used on the cover of the November 1920 issue of Fur News and Outdoor World.

References by Other Authors in Chronological Order

A Brief Account of the Wood Family in Virginia. M. B. Wood. 1893.

Rich Harvest Being Reaped by Huntsmen. The Republican-Journal. December 20, 1916.

Trapper Wins the $50.00 Prize with a "High Grip" Game Trap. Hunter Trader Trapper. May 1917.

Canning and Preserving the Surplus Products on the Farm. The Inland Farmer. Iris Summers. May 1, 1917.

Notes and Comments of Trade Interest. Fur News. R. K. Wood visits NYC. July 1917.

Holston News. Mid Methodist. July 17, 1918.

A Few Incidents of the Trap and Trail Line. Hunter Trader Trapper. E.J. Dailey. October 1917.

Two Bears. Fur News. Raymond Spears. December 1917.

Modern Traps and Trapping. Hunter Trader Trapper. E.J. Dailey. February 1918.

By-Products of the Trap Line. Fur News. F. E. Brimmer. August 1918.

How to Catch'em: Jim Smiley's Trap Line, VII. Marten I. Fur News. Raymond S. Spears. October 1918.

Good-Bye Old Trap Line. Hunter Trader Trapper. E.J. Dailey. November 1918.

Laws Relating to Fur-Bearing Animals, 1918. United States Department of Agriculture. Farmers' Bulletin 1022. December 1918.

Spring Rat Trapping and Other Things. Trapping Topics. Hunter Trader Trapper. E.J. Dailey. May 1919.

Auto Breaks Pole, Occupants Unhurt. Syracuse Journal. August 6, 1919.

Adirondack Region Timber Wolf Scare a Hoax. The Adirondack Record. February 27, 1920.

On a Backwoods Trapline. Hunter Trader Trapper. E.J. Dailey. May 1920.

The Observation Station: Wolf! Wolf! The Conservationist. New York State Conservation Commission. August, 1920.

The Adventures of Peter Unprime. Fur News. October 1920.

My Best Bet Trap Sets. Hunter Trader Trapper. F. E. Brimmer. January 1921.

Questions and Answers. Hunter Trader Trapper. January 1921.

Editors and Their Wants. Writer's Monthly. July 1921.

Corona Advertisement. Fur News and Outdoor World. July 1921.

Good Trapping Country, No .1, A Lot Depends on the Trapper. Hunter Trader Trapper. Raymond S. Spears. October 1921.

Fur Business is Booming. The Courier and Freeman, Potsdam, New York. December 21, 1921.

Out for Fur and Fun. Fur News and Outdoor World. E.J. Dailey. February 1922.

Spring Rat Trapping in New York. Hunter Trader Trapper. E.J. Dailey. April 1922

North Woods Trapping. Fur News and Outdoor World. E.J. Dailey. May 1922.

Questions and Answers. Hunter Trader Trapper. June 1922.

From the Editor's Tepee: Dick Wood has Hit the Trail and Trap Line Again. Fur News and Outdoor World. September 1922.

On the Trail of Sly Reynard. Fur News and Outdoor World. E.J. Dailey. October 1922.

When the Leaves Turn Gold. Fur News and Outdoor World. E.J. Dailey. November 1922.

Golden Days on the Trail and Trapline, Part I. Hunter Trader Trapper. E.J. Dailey. December 1922.

Golden Days on the Trail and Trapline, Part II. Hunter Trader Trapper. E.J. Dailey. January 1923.

Adirondack Trails. Hunter Trader Trapper. E.J. Dailey. February 1924.

Snow Trapping. Fur News and Outdoor World. E.J. Dailey. February 1925.

A. R. Harding Buys Fur News and Outdoor World. Fur News and Outdoor World. August 1925.

Perils of the Trail. Fur Fish Game. E.J. Dailey. January 1926.

Walter A. Gibbs vs Triumph Trap Company. Transcript of Record. US Circuit Court of Appeals. July 1926.

Sportsman to Cross State in Flimsy Canvas Boat. Knoxville News-Sentinel. June 14, 1927.

Life in the Trapper's Country. Fur Fish Game. E.J. Dailey. October 1928.

Richard Kennedy Wood. Who's Who among North American Authors Volume IV. 1929-1930.

Graflex Camera Advertisement. Popular Science Monthly. May 1930.

The Winter Trapline. Fur and Trapping. Sportsman's Digest. E.J. Dailey. December 1930.

Richard Kennedy Wood. Who's Who among North American Authors Volume V. 1931-1932.

Adirondacks Snow Trapping. Fur Fish Game. E.J. Dailey. February 1934.

My Jo-Indian Trapline. Fur Fish Game. E.J. Dailey. October 1934.

Trappers' Friend. Hill Bros. Fur Co. 1935-1936.

The Oswegatchie Trapline. Fur Fish Game. E.J Dailey. October 1936.

True History of ATA. Fur Fish Game. E.J. Dailey. November 1936.

Adirondack Reds. Hunter Trader Trapper. E.J. Dailey. December 1936.

Protection. Fur Fish Game. E.J. Dailey. December 1936.
How True is "True History"? North American Trapper. R.S. Oakes. December 1936.

Brother ATA Members. North American Trapper. R.S. Oakes. December 1936.

Dick Wood Edits Sports Department. Automobile and Trailer Travel. March 1937.

A Mixed Trapline. Fur Fish Game. E.J. Dailey. September 1938.

Learning About Foxes. Hunter Trader Trapper Outdoorsman. E.J. Dailey. October 1938.

Buick Clicks with Veteran Cameraman. Buick Forum. The Buick Magazine. June 1939.

Graflex Camera Advertisement. Life. June 26, 1939.

Meet Dick Wood, Chattanooga Photographer. Chattanooga Times, Sunday Magazine. September 15, 1940.

Outdoor Sportsman. Dick Wood Gets Rainbow. Chattanooga Times. Grover Rann. September 22, 1940.

Trout Fishing in Tellico Area is Enjoyable. The Chattanooga Times. T.J. Williams. May 16, 1943.

Our Indian Lake Trapline. The Trappers World. EJ Dailey. March 1947.

Outdoor Writers Set Alaska Trip. Chattanooga Times. August 14, 1947.

True Temper Crippled Shad Advertisement. Popular Science. June 1948.

Cherokees Mark Museum Opening. Chattanooga Times. December 5, 1948.

Pet Firearms of Dick Wood. Muzzle Blasts. May 1952.

Ansil Dailey Obituary. Syracuse Post Standard. August 24, 1965.

Scenic South. Mobile Oil Company. November 1966.

Outdoor Writers of America Convene at Georgia's Callaway Gardens. All Outdoors. Chattanooga News. E. T. Bales. June 30, 1968.

Scenic South. Mobile Oil Company. July - August 1968.

Trapper Recalls Plenty of Game on Fence River. Northern Michigan Outdoors. Forest L. Carter. January 31, 1969.

E.J. "Adirondack" Dailey. Fur Fish Game. Paul Peck. June 1973.

Richard K. Wood Obituary. Chattanooga Times. November 2, 1977.

A Tribute to Richard K. Wood. Outdoors Unlimited, OWAA Newsletter. January 1978.

The Trapper's Hall of Fame – E.J. Dailey. The Trapper. Tom Krause. June 1979.

Our Organized History. The Trapper. Tom Krause. July 1982.

The Steel Trap in North America. Richard Gerstell. 1985.

Big Moose Lake in the Adirondacks. The Big Moose Lake History Project. 2004.

Saltville, VA Dam Break and Flood, Dec 1924. GenDisasters.com. Stu Beitler. 2010.

Email from Michael Courtney, Outreach Librarian, Herman B. Wells Library, Indiana University. Photographs of Who's Who among North American Authors, Vol IV, VI and VII. April 12, 2016.

Email from Dr. Robert Allen, Archivist, Hardwick-Johnston Memorial Library, Hiwassee College. Richard Kennedy Wood - Bachelor of Science High School Degree. April 14, 2016.

History – Hiwassee College. http://hiwassee.edu/about-us/history/. Printed April 30, 2016.

Sketches of Holston Preachers.
http://holston.org/media/about/resource/sketches_of_Holston_Preachers.doc.
Printed April 30, 2016.

Email about Sam McGee Cabin. MacKenzie Downing. MacBride Museum of Yukon History. Dated July 5, 2016.

Email about Bill Wood. Jim Kammer. Public Historian. Hamlet of Racquette Lake. Dated July 6, 2016.

Wolf Caught in Duane. The Malone Farmer. January 28, 1920. Article retrieved from the Franklin County Historical and Museum Society on August 29, 2016.

The Heydays of the Adirondacks. Maitland C. De Sormo. 1974. Book retrieved from the Franklin County Historical and Museum Society on August 29, 2016.

John R. Spears Information. Biography Book – File Cabinet Q-S BK-2. Little Falls Historical Society Museum. Little Falls, New York. Information retrieved on August 30, 2016.

Do you Trap or Hunt? Farm and Fireside. October, Unknown year.

Peck's Quality Lures Brochure. E.H. Peckinpaugh Company, Chattanooga, Tennessee. Unknown year.

References by Dick Wood in Chronological Order
Don't Wink or Blink. All Outdoors. R. K. Wood. November 1915.

Kinks: A Book of 250 Helpful Hints for Hunters, Anglers and Outers. A Minnow Trap. Richard K. Wood. 1917.

Notes from Holston. Fur News. Richard K. Wood. March 1917.

Popular Fishing Outfits. Fur News. Richard K. Wood. July 1917.

Trapping for Muskrats and Getting Them. Fur News. Richard K. Wood. September 1917.

Successful Sets for Fur-Bearers. Our Boy Trappers. Farm Life. Richard K. Wood. November 1917.

Trapping Minks. Farm and Fireside. Richard K. Wood. November 17, 1917.

Trapping Skunks and Coons. Farm and Fireside. Richard K. Wood. December 1, 1917.

Make Your Trapping Pay. Our Boy Trappers. Farm Life. Richard K. Wood. December 1917.

Trapping the Fur Bearers. Farm and Home. Richard K. Wood. December 1917.

Trapping Days. Fur News. Richard K. Wood. December 1917.

Mink Trapping. Fur News. Richard K. Wood. December 1917.

Gripping the Dollars. Triumph Trap Company. Dick Wood. 1917.

Trapping Tricks for Common Furbearers. Triumph Trap Company. Dick Wood. 1918.

Modern Trapping Methods. Triumph Trap Company. Dick Wood. 1918.

Getting Clear Water from a Muddy Spring. Outer's Book – Recreation. Richard K. Wood. January 1918.

How To Catch 'Em: Triple Clutch – High Grip, The New Efficiency Trap. Richard K. Wood. Fur News. January 1918.

Pipe Dreams of a Gun Crank. Hunter Trader Trapper. Richard K. Wood. February 1918.

With Randall on the Boreas Part I. Fur News. Richard K. Wood. February 1918.

Tricks in Trapping Skunks. The Nebraska Farmer. Dick Wood. February 19, 1918.

With Randall on the Boreas Part II. Fur News. Richard K. Wood. March 1918.

Contemptible Practices. Fur News. R.K. Wood. March 1918.

The Trapper's Clothing. Woodcraft. Fur News. Richard K. Wood. April 1918.

Boots and Marshes Part One. Fur News. Richard K. Wood. May 1918.

Boots and Marshes Part Two. Fur News. Richard K. Wood. June 1918.

Trout, Wildcats and Rattlesnakes, Part One. Fur News. Richard K. Wood. July 1918.

Oneida Lake Fishing. Hunter Trader Trapper. Richard K. Wood. July 1918.

Trapping College Money. Hunter Trader Trapper. Dick Wood. August 1918.

The Camp Fire Girl's Camera and Its Use. Wohelo: Magazine of the Camp Fire Girls. Richard K. Wood. August 1918.

Trout, Wildcats and Rattlesnakes, Part Two. Fur News. Richard K. Wood. September 1918.

Lake Fishing. Fur News. R.K. Wood. September 1918.

Fur and Trapping. Family Herald Weekly Star, Montreal, Canada. Richard K. Wood. September 25, 1918.

Furs Will Be Popular. Farm and Home. Richard K. Wood. October 1918.

Fur Farming: Muskrat Farming. Fur News. R. K. Wood. October 1918.

The Lure of the Trap Line. The American Boy. Richard K. Wood. October 1918.

Trapping the Mink. The Nebraska Farmer. Richard K. Wood. October 12, 1918.

A Trapper's Musings: No. I - Musings. Fur News. Dick Wood. November 1918.

The Lure of the Trap Line, Second Article. The American Boy. Richard K. Wood. November 1918.

How to Hunt and Trap Animals. The Canadian Countryman. Richard K. Wood. November 9, 1918.

Trapping the Dollar Furs. The Nebraska Farmer. Richard K. Wood. November 9, 1918.

A Trapper's Musings: No. II - Trapping. Fur News. Dick Wood. December 1918.

Southern Trapping Conditions. Hunter Trader Trapper. Richard K. Wood. December 1918.

Trapping Tricks for Common Furbearers. Triumph Trap Company. Dick Wood. 1919.

A Trapper's Musings: No. III – The Mid-Winter Trap Line. Fur News. Dick Wood. January 1919.

Trapping the Skunk. The Country Gentleman. Richard K. Wood. January 11, 1919.

A Trapper's Musings: No. IV – Trappers. Fur News. Dick Wood. February 1919.

A Trapper's Musings: No. 6 – Dig 'Em Outs. Fur News. Dick Wood. March 1919.

A Trapper's Musings: No. VII – The Makings of a Trapper. Fur News. Dick Wood. April 1919.

A Trapper's Musings: No. VIII – The Victory Dance. Fur News. Dick Wood. May 1919.

Tripping the Wicomico, Chapter I. Fur News. Dick Wood. May 1919.

A Trapper's Musings: No. IX – King Nicotine. Fur News. Dick Wood. June 1919.

Tripping the Wicomico, Chapter II. Fur News. Dick Wood. June 1919.

Trouting in June. Fur News. Richard K. Wood. June 1919.

Muskrat Trapping on Marshes. Hunter Trader Trapper. Dick Wood. June 1919.

A Trapper's Musings: No. X – Master Rum. Fur News. Dick Wood. July 1919.

Tripping the Wicomico, Chapter III. Fur News. Dick Wood. July 1919.

Tripping the Wicomico, Chapter IV. Fur News. Dick Wood. August 1919.

A Trapper's Musings: No. 11 – Woman. Fur News. Dick Wood. August 1919.

A Trapper's Musings: No. XII – Fur Prospecting. Fur News. Dick Wood.
September 1919.

Tripping the Wicomico, Chapter V. Fur News. Dick Wood. September 1919.

The Pier Patrol. Fishing. Hunter Trader Trapper. Dick Wood. September 1919.

First Steps in Trapping. American Agriculturalist. Dick Farley. October 25,
1919.

Trapping the Million Dollar Furs. The Nebraska Farmer. Dick Wood.
November 29, 1919.

A Trapper's Musings: No. 11 – Trapping. Fur News. Dick Wood. December
1919.

Trapping Tricks for Common Furbearers. Triumph Trap Company. Dick Wood.
1920.

Traps and Tricks That Get the Furs. Dick Wood. 1920.

Modern Trapping Methods. Triumph Trap Company. Dick Wood. 1920.

Profitable Furs from Animals that Live Near By. Field and Stream. Dick Wood.
January 1920.

The February Trap Line. Fur News. Dick Wood. February 1920.

Luck Don't Count. Rod and Gun in Canada. Richard K. Wood. February 1920.

On the Fine Art of Fur Trapping. Forest and Stream. Richard K. Wood.
February 1920.

Trapping Wages on Home Ground. Fur News. Dick Wood. March 1920.

The New Order of Things. Fur News. Dick Wood. June 1920.

King Trout of the Boreas. The Boys' Magazine. Dick Wood. June 1920.

Finding Dare Buck of Hell Hole. Outers' Recreation. Richard K. Wood. July 1920.

Fishing Craft: The Gentle Art of Still Fishing. Fur News. Dick Wood. July 1920.

Fishing Craft: Trout – Two at a Crack. Fur News and Outdoor World. Dick Wood. August 1920.

Trappers' Equipment: Gunning for Guns. Fur News and Outdoor World. Dick Wood. August 1920.

Trappers' Equipment: The Trail Hiker's Outfit. Fur News and Outdoor World. Dick Wood. September 1920.

Fishing Craft: The Lure of the Bass Stream. Fur News and Outdoor World. Dick Wood. September 1920.

Leaping Bass of the Holston. Fishing. Hunter Trader Trapper. Dick Wood. September 1920.

Trappers' Equipment: Camps. Fur News and Outdoor World. Dick Wood. October 1920.

Trail Tested and Right. Fur News and Outdoor World. Dick Wood. October 1920.

A Trapper of the Oswegatchie. Fur News and Outdoor World. Dick Wood. November 1920.

Trail Tested and Right. Fur News and Outdoor World. Dick Wood. November 1920.

Trappers' Equipment: The Trapper's Belt. Fur News and Outdoor World. Dick Wood. November 1920.

The Fur Pocket on Seward, Part I. Farm Life. Richard K. Wood. November 1920.

The Big Moose Trap Line. Fur News and Outdoor World. Dick Wood. December 1920.

Trail Tested and Right. Fur News and Outdoor World. Dick Wood. December 1920.

Trappers' Equipment: Let There Be Light. Fur News and Outdoor World. Dick Wood. December 1920.

Land of Christmas Trees. Fur News and Outdoor World. Dick Wood. December 1920.

Trap Line Stunts on Land. The Sportsman's World. Field and Stream. Dick Wood. December 1920.

The Fur Pocket on Seward, Part II. Farm Life. Richard K. Wood. December 1920.

Cabin Life. Fur News and Outdoor World. Dick Wood. January 1921.

Beavers. Hartford Courant. Dick Wood. January 1921.

Trap Line Stunts – in the Water. The Sportsman's World. Field and Stream. Dick Wood. January 1921.

The Fur Pocket on Seward, Part III. Farm Life. Richard K. Wood. January 1921.

Pelts for Sale. The Sportsman's World. Field and Stream. Dick Wood. February 1921.

The Cold River Trail. Fur News and Outdoor World. Dick Wood. February 1921.

Trail Tested and Right: Stonebridge Folding Baker. Fur News and Outdoor World. Dick Wood. February 1921.

Trappers' Equipment: Tenting A La Hobo. Fur News and Outdoor World. Dick Wood. February 1921.

The Fur Pocket on Seward, Part IV. Farm Life. Richard K. Wood. February 1921.

Trappers' Equipment: The Life-Saver Kit. Fur News and Outdoor World. Dick Wood. March 1921.

Trail Tested and Right. Fur News and Outdoor World. Dick Wood. March 1921.

The Otter's Trail. Fur News and Outdoor World. Dick Wood. March 1921.

The Fur Pocket on Seward, Part V. Farm Life. Richard K. Wood. March 1921.

Trapping the Fisher. Hunter Trader Trapper. Adirondack Dick. April 1921.

The Picture is the Thing. Outers' Recreation. Richard K. Wood. May 1921.

New Trout Lures. Fur News and Outdoor World. Dick Wood. May 1921.

Trail Tested and Right. Fur News and Outdoor World. Dick Wood. May 1921.

Plugs for Bass. Fur News and Outdoor World. Dick Wood. June 1921.

Trail Tested and Right: Binoculars. Fur News and Outdoor World. Dick Wood. June 1921.

Deep Sea Fishing Off the Jersey Banks. Fur News and Outdoor World. Dick Wood. July 1921.

Trail Tested and Right: Pipe. Fur News and Outdoor World. Dick Wood. July 1921.

Prospecting Trapping Grounds. Fur News and Outdoor World. Dick Wood. October 1921.

Trap Line Togs. Hunter Trader Trapper. Dick Wood. October 1921.

Afoot in Deer Country. Fur News and Outdoor World. Dick Wood. November 1921.

Narratives of Trapping Life. Dick Wood. 1922.

Trapping as a Professional. Dick Wood. 1922.

My Visit to an Old Moonshiner's Home. Farm and Fireside. Richard K. Wood. January 1922.

Tips for the Photographer. The Target. Richard K. Wood. April 15, 1922.

Trapper's Lure. Western Story Magazine. Dick Wood. July 1922.

Pioneer Trappers and Hunters. Fur News and Outdoor World. Richard K. Wood. September 1922.

October Work on the Trapline. Fur News and Outdoor World. Dick Wood. October 1922.

The Trapper's Country: Part I. Fur News and Outdoor World. Dick Wood. December 1922.

The Trapper's Country: Part II. Fur News and Outdoor World. Dick Wood. January 1923.

Raccoons for the Amateur Fur Farmer. Fur News and Outdoor World. Dick Wood. January 1923.

The Trapper's Country: Part III. Fur News and Outdoor World. Dick Wood. February 1923.

The Trapper's Country: Part IV. Fur News and Outdoor World. Dick Wood. March 1923.

The Trapper's Country: Part V. Fur News and Outdoor World. Dick Wood. April 1923.

Canis Lupus, The Ferocious(?) Gray Wolf. Fur News and Outdoor World. Dick Wood. May 1923.

My Camera Outfit. Fur News and Outdoor World. Dick Wood. June 1923.

Rock Bass, Crappies, Perch and Cats. Fur News and Outdoor World. Dick Wood. July 1923.

Out-of-Doors. The Classmate. Dick Wood. July 21, 1923.

The Passenger Pigeon. Fur News and Outdoor World. Dick Wood. August 1923.

Go-Light Camping Outfits. Fur News and Outdoor World. Dick Wood. October 1923.

Our Popular Upland Game Birds. Fur News and Outdoor World. Dick Wood. November 1923.

Camping on the Trapline. Fur News and Outdoor World. Dick Wood. December 1923.

Handling Raw Furs – The Fur Outlook. American Agriculturist. Dick DuBois. December 8, 1923.

Trapping on Snow and Under Ice. Fur News and Outdoor World. Dick Wood. January 1924.

Winter Camping and Tramping. The Classmate. Dick Wood. January 12, 1924.
Beaver Trapping – Past and Present. Fur News and Outdoor World. Dick Wood. February 1924.

Snowshoes. The Classmate. Dick Wood. February 2, 1924.

Woodcraft: My Favorite Knives. Fur News and Outdoor World. Dick Wood. March 1924.

The Restless Otter. Fur News and Outdoor World. Dick Wood. April 1924.

Trout Streams Par Excellence. Fur News and Outdoor World. Dick Wood. May 1924.

Bass Fishing Tackle and Methods. Fur News and Outdoor World. Dick Wood. June 1924.

Bait and Flies for Trout. The Classmate. Dick Wood. June 7, 1924.

Outfitting for Hiking Trips: Part I. Fur News and Outdoor World. Dick Wood. July 1924.

The Large-Mouth Black Bass. The Classmate. Dick Wood. July 12, 1924.

Small-Mouth Black Bass. The Classmate. Dick Wood. July 19, 1924.

Outfitting for Hiking Trips: Part II. Fur News and Outdoor World. Dick Wood. August 1924.

Logs of Early Western Travelers. The Classmate. Dick Wood. August 23, 1924.

Bass, Pike, and Cats. Fur News and Outdoor World. Dick Wood. September 1924.

Go LIGHT Motor Camping. Motor Camper and Tourist. Dick Wood. September 1924.

How To Catch 'Em: Why I Use Blind Sets in the Fall. Fur News and Outdoor World. Dick Wood. October 1924.

Woodcraft: Woodcraft for Trappers. Fur News and Outdoor World. Dick Wood. November 1924.
Once around the Trap Line. Successful Farming. Dick Wood. November 1924.

Motoring into Dixie Land. Motor Trails and Camp Life. Outing. Richard K. Wood. November 1924.

South Bend Quality Tackle. Fishing – What Baits and When. Richard K. Wood. 1925.

Trapping Sly Foot: The Mink. Farm Journal. Dick Wood. January 1925.

Trapping as a Side Line. American Agriculturist. Richard K. Wood. January 17, 1925.

Winter Trapping of Muskrats in Northern New York. American Agriculturist. Richard K. Wood. January 17, 1925.

Winter Touring the Adirondacks Part 1. Motor Trails and Camp Life. Outing. Richard K. Wood. February 1925.

Winter Touring the Adirondacks Part 2. Motor Trails and Camp Life. Outing. Richard K. Wood. March 1925.

Northward Trek. Motor Camper and Tourist. Richard K Wood. July 1925.

The Camera for a Vacation. The Classmate. Richard K. Wood. July 4, 1925.

Touring and Camping through the Adirondacks. Sportlife. Richard K. Wood. September 1925.

The Trap Line in the Coulee. Successful Farming. Dick Wood. October 1925.

Snow Trapping. Farm and Fireside. Dick Wood. December 1925.

The Winter Trapline. Fur Fish Game. Dick Wood. January 1926.

The Elbow Lake Trapper. Farm, Stock and Home/Northwest Farmstead. Dick Wood. January 15, 1926.

Famous Trappers I Have Known – Bill Randall. Fur Fish Game. Dick Wood. February 1926.

Hunting Wild Animals in Michigan. True Western Stories. Richard K. Wood. March 1926.

In the Open. Motor Camper and Tourist. Richard K. Wood. May 1926.

Pioneer Spirit Still Lives in North Woods. Fawcett's Triple-X Magazine. Richard K. Woods. May 1926.

Outfitting for a Canoe Trip. Field and Stream. Richard K. Wood. June 1926.

Vacation a la Canoe, Part One. The Classmate. Richard K. Wood. July 10, 1926.

Vacation a la Canoe, Part Two. The Classmate. Richard K. Wood. July 17, 1926.

Is the Grey Wolf Dangerous? Wild Game Stories. Dick Wood. May-June 1926.

It Was Cheaper Than Staying Home. Farm and Fireside. Dick Wood. June 1926.

What New York State Offers the Motor Camper. Motor Camper & Tourist. Richard K. Wood. August 1926.

The Pocket Camera and Its Accessories. The Classmate. Richard K. Wood. August 11, 1926.

How I became a Fur Trader. Wild Game Stories. Dick Wood. September 1926.

Rawhide Thongs. Wild Game Stories. Dick Wood. September 1926.

An Old-Timer Showed Me These Trapping Tricks. Farm and Fireside. Dick Wood. October 1926.

Tanning Buckskin – Indian Method. Wild Game Stories. Richard K. Wood. November 1926.

To Tent and Camp Equipment Manufacturers. National Sportsman. Dick Wood. 1926.

Shake Hands with Dick Wood. Motor Camping Department. National Sportsman. Dick Wood. November 1926.

The Rainbows of Little Pigeon. National Sportsman. Dick Wood. November 1926.

Ozark Playgrounds. National Sportsman. Dick Wood. November 1926.

Bill Was the Best Trapper I Ever Knew. Farm and Fireside. Dick Wood. December 1926.

My Old Hen Bait. Farm and Fireside. Dick Wood. January 1927.

Reelfoot Lake – A Sportsman's Paradise. National Sportsman. Dick Wood. February 1927.

Florida – The Angler's Mecca. Motor Camping Department. National Sportsman. March 1927.

Motoring to Trouting Waters. Motor Camping Department. National Sportsman. Dick Wood. May 1927.

The Land of the Sky. Motor Camping Department. National Sportsman. Dick Wood. June 1927.

Virginia's Scenic Attractions. Motor Camping Department. National Sportsman. Dick Wood. July 1927.

A Compact Hiking Kit. The Classmate. Richard K. Wood. July 9, 1927.

The Bass Fisherman on Tour. National Sportsman. Dick Wood. August 1927.

Catching Trap-Shy Mink and Muskrat. The Farm Journal. Dick Wood. December 1927.

Trapping Tricks Old Eli Taught Me. Farm and Fireside. Dick Wood. December 1927.

My Muskrat Sets. Farm and Fireside. Dick Wood. January 1928.

Furnishing the Portable Camp. Motor Camping Department. National Sportsman. Dick Wood. March 1928.

The Automatic Reel. Pools and Ripples. A Department for Fishermen. National Sportsman. Dick Wood. March 1928.

Proving the Outboard in Fast Water. National Sportsman. Dick Wood. March 1928.

Lure of the Ozark Trails. Motor Camping Department. National Sportsman. Dick Wood. April 1928.

The Outdoorsman's Eyes. National Sportsman. Dick Wood. June 1928.

A Life Saver Kit. National Sportsman. Dick Wood. June 1928.

The Small Car Camping Outfit. Motor Camping Department. National Sportsman. Dick Wood. September 1928.

Tag End of Trout Season. Pools and Ripples. A Department for Fishermen. National Sportsman. Dick Wood. September 1928.

Adirondack Trap Trails. Hunting and Fishing. Lon Baker. October 1928.

Yellowstone. National Sportsman. Dick Wood. November 1928.

Furnishing the Camp Trailer. Motor Camping Department. National Sportsman. Dick Wood. November 1928.

Fighting Barracuda. Pools and Ripples. A Department for Fishermen. National Sportsman. Dick Wood. November 1928.

First Aid for Hunters and Campers. Hunting and Fishing. Dick Wood. November 1928.

Take Along an Outboard. Motor Camping Department. National Sportsman. Dick Wood. December 1928.

The Five Kingfishers. Pools and Ripples. A Department for Fishermen. National Sportsman. Dick Wood. December 1928.

The Treasure Book. Herskovits. Dick Wood. 1929.

The Winter Camper. Motor Camping Department. National Sportsman. Dick Wood. January 1929.

The 1929 Motor Tourist. Motor Camping Department. National Sportsman. Dick Wood. February 1929.

Equipping the Tourist. Motor Camping Department. National Sportsman. Dick Wood. March 1929.

What Brains Did With Ninety Acres of Wild Land. The Southern Planter. Richard K. Wood. March 1, 1929.

Into the West. Motor Camping Department. National Sportsman. Dick Wood. April 1929.

Rambling Through Minnesota. Motor Camping Department. National Sportsman. Dick Wood. May 1929.

Colorado's Motor Trails. Motor Camping Department. National Sportsman. Dick Wood. June 1929.

Perfect Vacations in Motor Touring. Outdoors. Physical Culture. June 1929.

Where Motor Trails End. Motor Camping Department. National Sportsman. Dick Wood. August 1929.

Fishing for Health – and Fish. Outdoors. Physical Culture. Richard K. Wood. August 1929.

The Passing of the Bison. Hunter Trader Trapper. Dick Wood. September 1929.

The Smiling Ozarks. Motor Camping Department. National Sportsman. Dick Wood. September 1929.

The Blanket an' Skillet Camper. Motor Camping Department. National Sportsman. Dick Wood. October 1929.

The Fur Trapper's Life. Sportsman's Digest. Dick Wood. October 1929.

Trappers' Queries. The Farm Journal. Dick Wood. October 1929.

Camp Stoves, Cooking Kits and Kitchenettes. Motor Camping Department. National Sportsman. Dick Wood. November 1929.

Trapping Hints. The Farm Journal. Dick Wood. November 1929.

The Long Trail West. Motor Camping Department. National Sportsman. Dick Wood. December 1929.

Trapping Queries. The Farm Journal. Dick Wood. December 1929.

Animal Tracks Lead to Pelt Money. The Farm Journal. Richard K. Wood. January 1930.

The Trapper Afloat. Hunter Trader Trapper. Dick Wood. January 1930.

Stalking Wolves. Far West Stories. Richard K. Wood. February 1930.

Outboards for Sportsmen. Hunter Trader Trapper. Richard K. Wood. March 1930.

The Crappie, Prince of Pan Fish. Sportsman's Digest. Richard K. Wood. March 1930.

The Angler: Black Bass. Mid-West Sportsman. Dick Wood. April 1930.

Tigers of the Sea. Hunter Trader Trapper. Richard K. Wood. May 1930.

How Do You Sleep? National Sportsman. Dick Wood. May 1930.

An Easy Towing Boat Trailer. Popular Science Monthly. Dick Wood. June 1930.

Outfitting for the Cruise. Outboard Motor Boat and Popular Boating. Dick Wood. June 1930.

The Angler: Panfish. Mid-West Sportsman. Dick Wood. June-July 1930.

The Outdoor Cooking-Fire. Young People's Paper. Dick Wood. July 5, 1930.

Cooking Meats in Camp. Young People's Paper. Dick Wood. July 12, 1930.

The Angler's Choice. Sportsman's Digest. Richard K. Wood. July-August 1930.

Big Bass of Ocklawaha. Hunter Trader Trapper. Dick Wood. September 1930.

Musky Lore. Field and Stream. Dick Wood. September 1930.

A Trapper's Close Call. Sports Afield. Dick Dubois. November 1930.

Outdoors with a Camera, Part One. Sports Afield. Richard K. Wood. November 1930.

In The Winter Woods, Part One. Sportsman's Digest. Dick Wood. November 1930.

Outdoors with a Camera, Part Two. Sports Afield. Richard K. Wood. December 1930.

In The Winter Woods, Part Two. Sportsman's Digest. Dick Wood. December 1930.

Outdoors with a Camera, Part III. Sports Afield. Richard K Wood. January 1931.

The Peninsula Wolfer. Sportsman's Digest. Dick Dubois. December 1931.

Near Wilderness Trapping. Comfort Magazine. Dick Wood. December 1931.

Before the Snow Flies. Hunter Trader Trapper. Dick Wood. January 1932.

The Modern Beaver Hunters. Hunter Trader Trapper. Dick Wood. March 1932.

A Tennessee River Duck Hunt. Fur Fish Game. Dick Wood. January 1933.

Luck on Phoenix Run. Hunter Trader Trapper. Richard K. Wood. April 1933.

The Art of Fly Casting. The Target. Dick Wood. June 3, 1933.

Musquash of the Marshes. The Young People's Paper. Dick Wood. June 18, 1933.
In the Southern Highlands. The Classmate. Richard K. Wood. June 24, 1933.

Paddling Your Canoe. The Target. Richard K. Wood. August 19, 1933.

A Camp Kitchenette. The Michigan Sportsman. Dick Wood. September 1933.

Here is a Good Place for October Pike Fishing. ESSO Tours and Detours. Dick Wood. October 1933.

Methods of Famous Trappers Disclosed – advertisement. American Trapper. Dick Wood. 1934.

Walter M. Cline – Photographer of the South. The Commercial Photographer. Richard K. Wood. April 1934.

Virginia Bass Fishing. Hunter Trader Trapper. Dick Wood. April 1934.

Let's Go Fishin'. Esso Tours and Detours. Dick Wood. May 1934.

Camping is a Sport. Motor Touring and Camping. Sports Afield. Dick Wood. January 1935.

The Canoeing Outfit. Fur Fish Game. Dick Wood. April 1935.

My Favorite Motor Camping Tent. Motor Touring and Camping. Sports Afield. Dick Wood. May 1935.

Touring Afoot. Motor Touring and Camping. Sports Afield. Dick Wood. June 1935

Fortunes from Furs. Rural Progress Magazine. Dick Wood. December 1935.

Trapping for Profit and Game Protection. Game Breeder and Sportsman. Dick Wood. January 1936.

Bucking "Buck Fever" and the Bucks. American Motorist. Richard K. Wood. January 1936.

Fresh Water Fishing Adds New Thrills. American Motorist. Richard K. Wood. February, 1936.

Canoe and Camera. Hunting and Fishing in Canada. Dick Wood. February 1936.

Trout Streams of the Smokies. American Motorist. Richard K. Wood. May 1936.

Stoves for the Trailer Coach. Trailer Travel and Woodcraft. Sports Afield. Richard K. Wood. June 1936.

Lights for the Camper. Trailer Travel and Woodcraft. Sports Afield. Richard K. Wood. September 1936.

A Sportsman's Optical Equipment. Game Breeder and Sportsman. Dick Wood. September 1936.

Santeetlah Bass. The Trailer Caravan. Dick Wood. October 1936.

Outdoor Sports on the Caravan Trail. The Trailer Caravan. Dick Wood. October 1936.

Trailer Camping in Deer Country. The Trailer Caravan. Dick Wood. November-December 1936.

Outdoor Sports on the Caravan Trail. The Trailer Caravan. Dick Wood. November-December 1936.

This Bugaboo of Fox Trapping. Hunter Trader Trapper. Dick Wood. January 1937.

Greetings American Trapper's Protective Association Members. Fur Fish Game. Richard K. Wood. January 1937.

Now! The Trailers for 1937. Trailer Travel and Woodcraft. Sports Afield. Richard K. Wood. January 1937.

The 1937 Trailer Parade Continues. Trailer Travel and Woodcraft. Sports Afield. Richard K. Wood. February 1937.

The Lure of the Trout Streams. Hunting Fishing Sports. Automobile and Trailer Travel. Dick Wood. April 1937.

Build Your Own Trailer. Trailer Travel and Woodcraft. Sports Afield. Richard K. Wood. May 1937.

Regarding the Galley of the Modern Trailer. Trailer Travel and Woodcraft. Sports Afield. Richard K. Wood. July 1937.

How Safe Is Trailer Travel? Trailer Travel and Woodcraft. Sports Afield. Richard K. Wood. August 1937.

Outdoor Trails for Sport and Health. The Lone Ranger Magazine. Dick Wood. November 1937.

Tennessee Outdoors. Hunting Fishing Sports. Automobile and Trailer Travel. Dick Wood. December 1937.

The Baby Reflex. The Sportsman's Camera. National Sportsman. R. K. Wood. December 1937.

Camping on Fishing Trips. Camping and Woodcraft. Sports Afield Fishing Annual. Richard K. Wood. 1938.

The Sportsman's Camera. National Sportsman. Richard K. Wood. January 1938.

The Trailer and Winter Sports. Hunting Fishing Sports. Automobile and Trailer Travel. Dick Wood. February 1938.

Pictures – Day or Night. The Sportsman's Camera. National Sportsman. R. K. Wood. February 1938.

Starting Fires in Cold Weather. Trailer Travel and Woodcraft. Sports Afield. Richard K. Wood. February 1938.

Some Outdoor Meals. Trailer Travel and Woodcraft. Sports Afield. Richard K. Wood. March 1938.

Woodsmen and Woodcraft. Star Western. Dick Wood. April 1938.

New York Outdoors. Hunting Fishing Sports. Automobile and Trailer Travel. Dick Wood. July 1938.

Small-Mouths of the North Fork. Outdoors. Dick Wood. July 1939.

Professional Results with Small Cameras. American Photography. Richard K. Wood. January 1940.

What Camera for the Sportsman: The Larger Cameras. Hunting and Fishing. Richard K. Wood. October 1940.
Camp, Trail and Canoe. Outdoorsman Handbook Series. Dick Wood. 1941.

Compose your Picture. National Sportsman. Dick Wood. January 1941.

Synchro-Sunlight Photography. Hunting and Fishing. Richard K. Wood. May 1941.

Developing Your Own. Camera Department. National Sportsman. Richard K. Wood. October 1941.

Our Last Frontier. Everybody's Weekly, Philadelphia Inquirer. Richard K. Wood. January 25, 1948.

Air Hop Over North Ontario Bush Takes One to Cozy Camp. The Chattanooga Times. Dick Wood. August 28, 1949.

Singing the Blues. Hunting and Fishing. Dick Wood. August 1952.

Kokadjo Landlocks Save the Day. Unpublished. Dick Wood. 1966.

Paradise That Was. Georgia Game and Fish. Dick Wood. June 1971.

References by Dick Wood with Unknown Components in Alphabetical Order

A Camping Car de Luxe. The Target. Richard K. Wood. Unknown Date.

A Home-Made Line Drier. Outer's Book – Recreation. Richard K. Wood. Unknown Date.

A Hunters Jinrikisha. Field and Stream. Richard K. Wood. Unknown Date.

Adirondack Beavers. National Sportsman. Dick Wood. Unknown Date.

A Spring Hike in Northland. The Boys' Magazine. Dick Wood. Unknown Date.

Back of Horseshoe Bend. Sportsman's Digest. Richard K. Wood. Unknown Date.

Bannock and Other Camp-Dishes. Unknown Publication. Dick Wood. Unknown Date.

Bass the Universal Fish. Sportsman's Digest. Richard K. Wood. Unknown Date.

Binoculars. Outdoor Sports and Recreation. Chattanooga News. Dick Wood. Unknown Date.

Black Fox Farming. Furs and Hides. Unknown Publication. Richard K. Wood. Unknown Date.

Camouflaging the Fur Bearers, Part I. Unknown Publication. Richard K. Wood. 1918.

Camouflaging the Fur Bearers, Part II. Unknown Publication. Richard K. Wood. 1918.

Canoe and Camera. Outdoor Photography. National Sportsman. Dick Wood. Unknown Date.

Dick Farley's Trapping Partner. Sportsman's Digest. Dick Wood. Unknown Date.

Dry Fly Methods for Sly Trout. Outdoor Sports and Recreation. Chattanooga News. Dick Wood. Unknown Date.

First-Aid Kits for Campers and Hikers. Unknown Publication. Richard K. Wood. Unknown Date.

Following the Fur Trail Trap Line. The Boys' Magazine. Dick Wood. Unknown Date.

Hairbreadth Escapes from Wild Animals. Unknown Publication. Dick Wood. Unknown Date.

Hot Weather Pictures. Outdoor Photography. National Sportsman. Dick Wood. Unknown Date.

How and Where to Fish. Unknown Publication. Richard K. Wood. July 1926.

How We Caught Them. Dick Wood. Farm and Fireside. Unknown Date.

In the Shadow of the Smokies. Outdoor Recreation. Richard K. Wood. Unknown Date.

In the Woodland Ways. Unknown Publication. Dick Wood. Unknown Date.

Lanagan on Indian River, Missouri. Unknown Publication. Richard K. Wood. Unknown Date.

Musky Fishing. Outdoor Sports and Recreation. Chattanooga News. Dick Wood. Unknown Date.

My Camera Made a Man of Me. Graflex Advertisement. Physical Culture. Richard K. Wood. Unknown Date.

On Santeetlah Lake. Outdoor Sports and Recreation. Chattanooga News. Dick Wood. Unknown Date.

Outdoor Photography. Outdoor Sports and Recreation. Chattanooga News. Dick Wood. Unknown Date.

Outdoor Photography, Part One – The Outfit. Unknown Publication. Richard K. Wood. Unknown Date.

Outdoor Photography, Part Two – Successful Picture Making. Unknown Publication. Richard K. Wood. Unknown Date.

Pictures in the Snow. Hunting and Fishing. Dick Wood. Unknown Date.

Pin Money for Farm Boys. Unknown Publication. Richard K. Wood. Unknown Date.

Photo Trapping Methods. Dick Wood. Unknown Date.

Possibilities in Raising Rabbits. Sportsman's Digest. Dick Wood. Unknown Date.

Reelfoot Lake, Tennessee. Unknown Publication. Richard K. Wood. Unknown Date.

River Cruising in an Acme. Dick Wood. Unknown Date.

Silhouette Your Subject. Outdoor Photography. National Sportsman. Dick Wood. Unknown Date.

Successful Methods of Trapping. People's Popular Monthly. Richard K. Wood. Unknown Date.

Swimming. Outdoor Sports and Recreation. Chattanooga News. Dick Wood. Unknown Date.

The Trapper's School. The Household Journal. Richard K. Wood. October, Unknown Year.

The Trapper's School. The Household Journal. Richard K. Wood. November, Unknown Year.

Trail Wise. Outdoor Sports and Recreation. Chattanooga News. Dick Wood. Unknown Date.

Trap Lines and Deer Trails. Sportsman's Digest. Dick Wood. Unknown Date.

Trapping the Coyote. Unknown Publication. Richard K. Wood. Unknown Date.

Trout Stream Pictures. Outdoor Photography. National Sportsman. Dick Wood. Unknown Date.

Watch Your Exposure. How to Make Good Pictures. National Sportsman. Dick Wood. Unknown Date.

Walking Tours. Outdoor Sports and Recreation. Chattanooga News. Dick Wood. Unknown Date.

Ways of Fur Bearers. Southern Ruralist. R. K. Wood. Unknown Date.

Winter Woods Travel. The Target. Dick Wood. Unknown Date.

Woodchucks are a Pest. Unknown Publication. Richard K. Wood. Unknown Date.

Your Camera on Hunting Trips. National Sportsman. Dick Wood. Unknown Date.

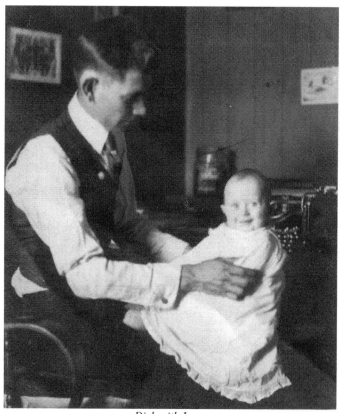

Dick with Inez.